Hal•Leonard ESSENTIAL SONGS

Contemporary Christian

PIANO VOCAL GUITAR

ISBN 978-1-4234-8062-4

7777 W. BLUEMOUND RD. P.O. BOX 13819 MILWAUKEE, WI 53213

For all works contained herein:
Unauthorized copying, arranging, adapting, recording, Internet posting, public performance,
or other distribution of the printed music in this publication is an infringement of copyright.
Infringers are liable under the law.

Visit Hal Leonard Online at
www.halleonard.com

CONTENTS

4	Awesome God	Rich Mullins
8	Beautiful	Audio Adrenaline
14	Brave	Nichole Nordeman
25	Bring the Rain	MercyMe
32	By His Wounds	Glory Revealed
38	Creed (Credo)	Third Day, Rich Mullins
58	Dive	Steven Curtis Chapman
49	East to West	Casting Crowns
66	El Shaddai	Amy Grant
72	Everything Glorious	David Crowder*Band
78	Fool for You	Nichole Nordeman
86	Get Down	Audio Adrenaline
92	Give Me Your Eyes	Brandon Heath
106	God Is in Control	Twila Paris
114	Hunger and Thirst	Susan Ashton
120	I Still Believe	Jeremy Camp
128	I Want to Be Just Like You	Phillips, Craig & Dean
99	I'm Not Alright	Sanctus Real
138	If I Stand	Rich Mullins
143	Joy	Newsboys
150	Knockin' on Heaven's Door	Avalon
159	Lead Me On	Amy Grant
177	Learning to Breathe	Switchfoot
168	Legacy	Nichole Nordeman
186	Let It Fade	Jeremy Camp
194	Let Us Pray	Steven Curtis Chapman

208	Lose My Soul	tobyMac featuring Kirk Franklin and Mandisa
201	More	Matthew West
218	My Will	dc Talk
225	No Better Place	Steven Curtis Chapman
232	Nothing Compares	Third Day
238	People Need the Lord	Steve Green
242	Place in This World	Michael W. Smith
247	Praise You in This Storm	Casting Crowns
254	Real to Me	Nichole Nordeman
261	Revolutionary Love	David Crowder*Band
268	Saving Grace	Point of Grace
284	Sea of Faces	Kutless
290	Secret Ambition	Michael W. Smith
298	Shine	Newsboys
275	Sing a Song	Third Day
304	Sometimes by Step	Rich Mullins
316	Song of Love	Rebecca St. James
322	Spoken For	MercyMe
309	Steady On	Point of Grace
328	This Is Your Life	Switchfoot
342	This Man	Jeremy Camp
337	Undo	Rush of Fools
350	Voice of Truth	Casting Crowns
360	We Need Jesus	Petra
376	What If I Stumble	dc Talk
386	Whatever You're Doing (Something Heavenly)	Sanctus Real
367	Wonder Why	Avalon
394	You Are the Answer	Point of Grace

AWESOME GOD

Words and Music by
RICH MULLINS

BEAUTIFUL

Words and Music by MARK STUART, WILL McGINNISS, BOB HERDMAN, TYLER BURKUM and BEN CISSELL

© 2001 UP IN THE MIX MUSIC (BMI), FLICKER USA PUBLISHING (BMI) and ALLEN VAUGHN AND RAY PUBLISHING (ASCAP)
Admin. by EMI CMG PUBLISHING
All Rights Reserved   Used by Permission

BRAVE

Words by NICHOLE NORDEMAN
Music by NICHOLE NORDEMAN and JAY JOYCE

BRING THE RAIN

Words and Music by BART MILLARD, BARRY GRAUL,
JIM BRYSON, NATHAN COCHRAN,
MIKE SCHEUCHZER and ROBBY SHAFFER

© 2006 Simpleville Music (ASCAP) and Wet As A Fish Music (ASCAP)
All Rights Administered by Simpleville Music, Inc.
All Rights Reserved   Used by Permission

BY HIS WOUNDS

Words and Music by MAC POWELL
and DAVID NASSER

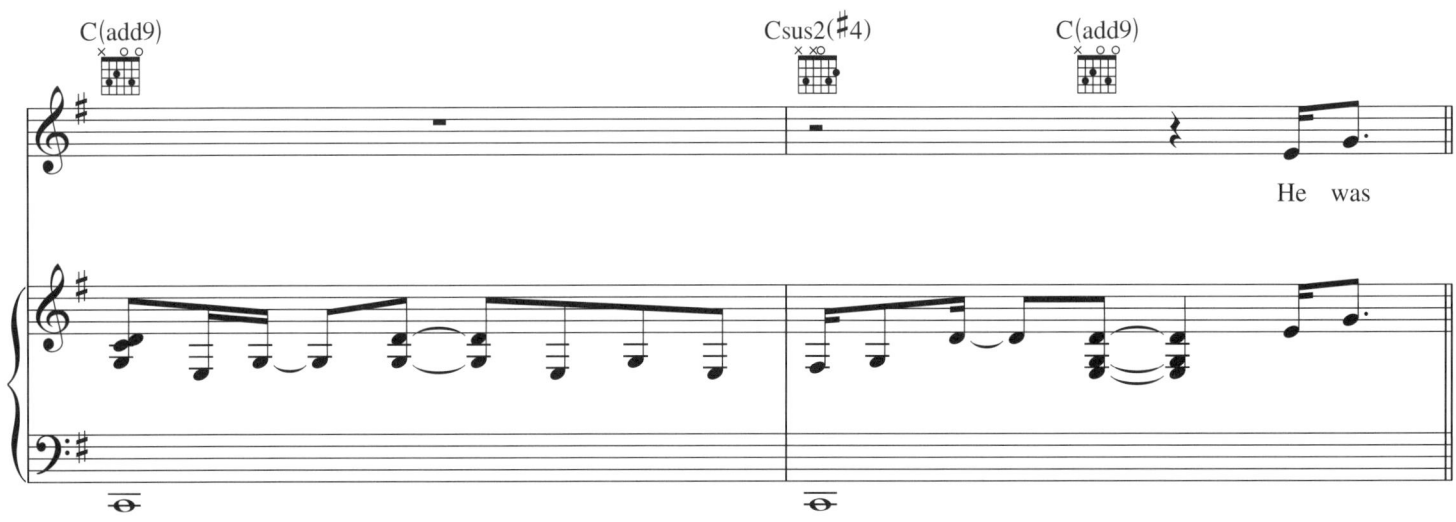

© 2007 MEAUX MERCY (BMI), CONSUMING FIRE MUSIC (ASCAP) and REDEMPTIVE ART MUSIC (BMI)
Admin. by EMI CMG PUBLISHING
All Rights Reserved   Used by Permission

CREED
(Credo)

Words and Music by
DAVID "BEAKER" STRASSER

EAST TO WEST

Words and Music by MARK HALL
and BERNIE HERMS

Moderate Rock beat

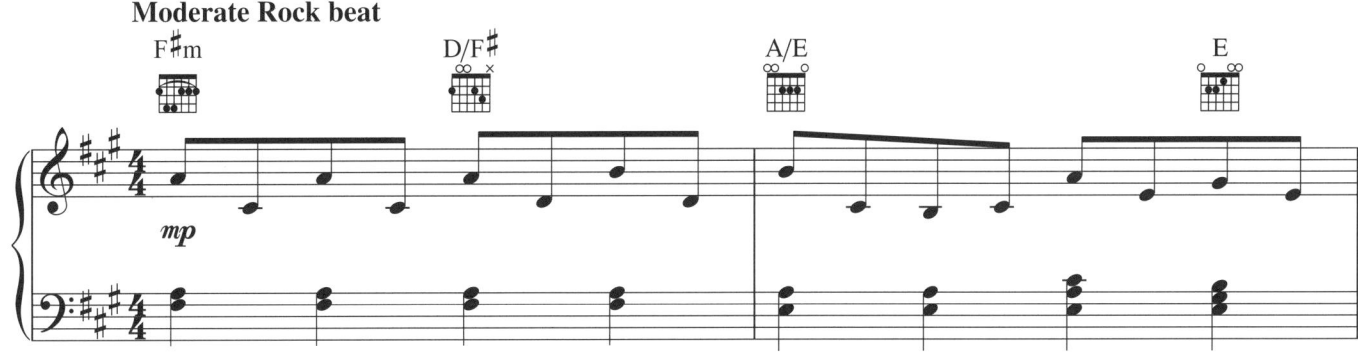

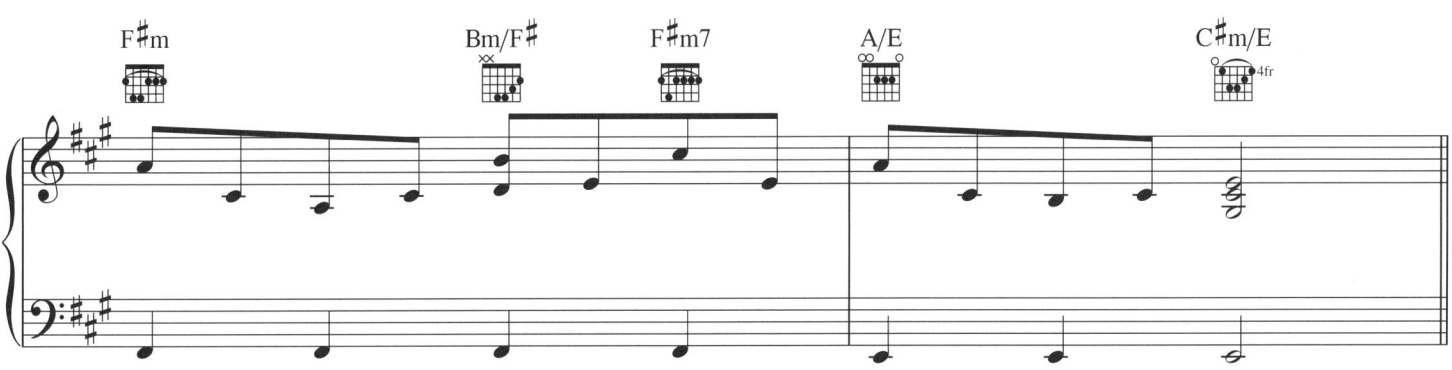

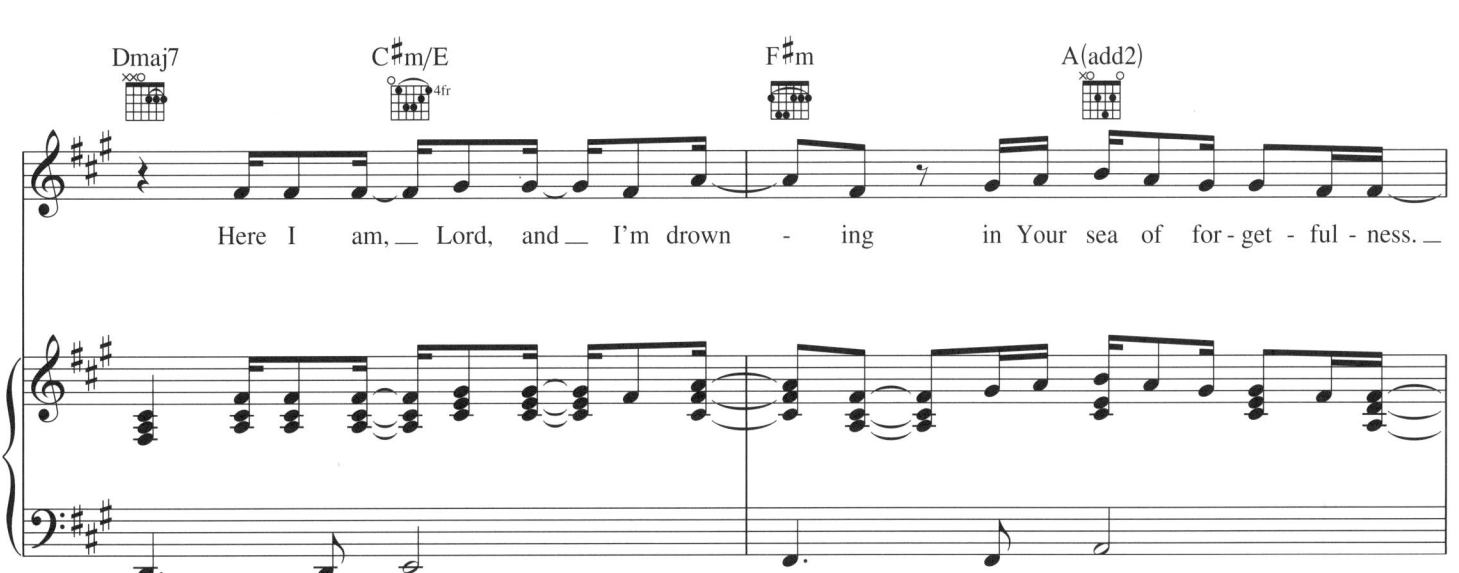

Here I am,__ Lord, and__ I'm drown- ing in Your sea of for-get-ful-ness.__

© 2007 MY REFUGE PUBLISHING (BMI), CLUB ZOO MUSIC (BMI), SWECS MUSIC (BMI), Word Music, LLC (ASCAP) and BANAHAMA TUNES (ASCAP)
MY REFUGE PUBLISHING, CLUB ZOO MUSIC and SWECS MUSIC Admin. by EMI CMG PUBLISHING
BANAHAMA TUNES Admin. by WORD MUSIC, LLC
All Rights Reserved   Used by Permission

DIVE

Words and Music by
STEVEN CURTIS CHAPMAN

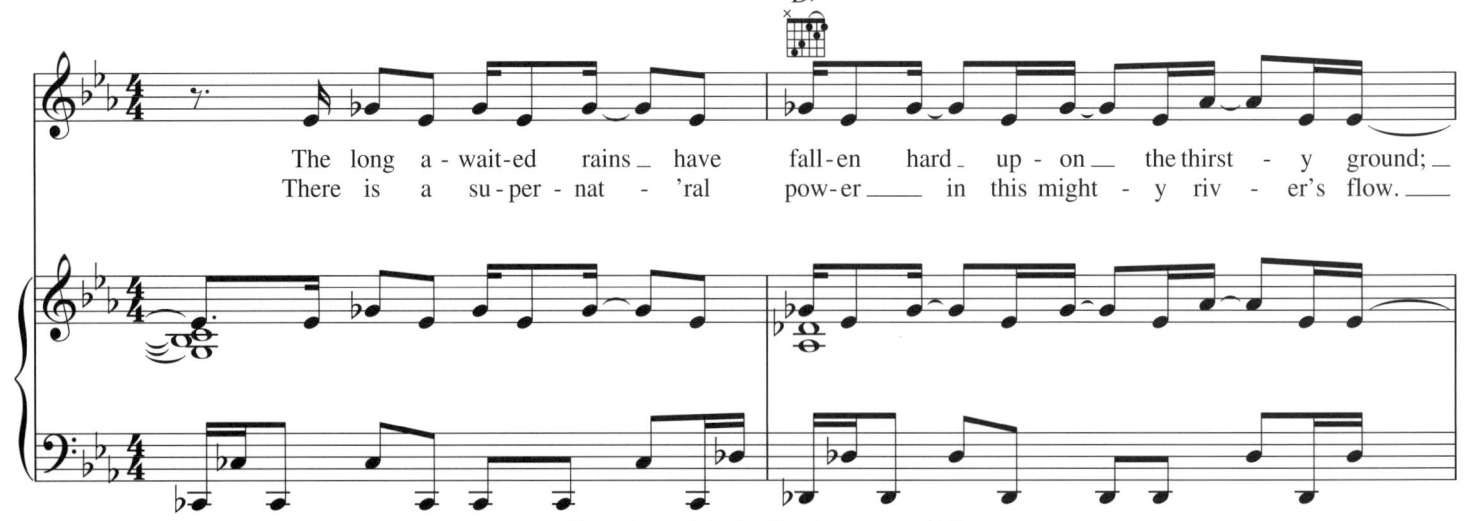

The long a-wait-ed rains_ have fall-en hard_ up-on_ the thirst-y ground;_
There is a su-per-nat-'ral pow-er_ in this might-y riv-er's flow._

© 1999 SPARROW SONG (BMI) and PEACH HILL SONGS (BMI)
Admin. by EMI CMG PUBLISHING
All Rights Reserved   Used by Permission

EVERYTHING GLORIOUS

Words and Music by
DAVID CROWDER

Moderately

The day is bright-er here with You.
My eyes are small, but they have seen

The night is light-er than its hue
the beau-ty of e-nor-mous things,

would lead me to be-lieve,
which leads me to be-lieve

which leads me to
there's light e-nough

* Recorded a half step lower.

© 2006 WORSHIPTOGETHER.COM SONGS (ASCAP) and sixsteps Music (ASCAP)
Admin. by EMI CMG PUBLISHING
All Rights Reserved   Used by Permission

GET DOWN

Words and Music by MARK STUART,
WILL McGINNISS, BOB HERDMAN,
TYLER BURKUM and BEN CISSELL

Moderately fast

(Verse)
Lav-ish-ly our lives are wast-ed; hum-ble-ness is left un-tast-ed.
All I need's an-oth-er day where I can't seem to get a-way

You can't live your life to please your-self, yeah.
from the man-y things that drag me down, yeah. I'm

© 1999 UP IN THE MIX MUSIC (BMI), FLICKER USA PUBLISHING (BMI) and ALLEN VAUGHN AND RAY PUBLISHING (ASCAP)
Admin. by EMI CMG PUBLISHING
All Rights Reserved   Used by Permission

I'M NOT ALRIGHT

Words and Music by DOUGLAS CAINE McKELVEY,
MATT HAMMITT, CHRIS ROHMAN, MARK GRAALMAN,
CHRIS STEVENS and DAN GARTLEY

*Recorded a half step lower.

© 2006 BIRDWING MUSIC (ASCAP), GOTEE MUSIC (BMI), REGISFUNK MUSIC (BMI), RIVER OAKS MUSIC COMPANY (BMI) and SONGS WITHOUT BORDERS (SESAC)
BIRDWING MUSIC, GOTEE MUSIC, REGISFUNK MUSIC and RIVER OAKS MUSIC COMPANY Admin. by EMI CMG PUBLISHING
SONGS WITHOUT BORDERS Admin. by SIMPLEVILLE MUSIC, INC.
All Rights Reserved   Used by Permission

GOD IS IN CONTROL

Words and Music by
TWILA PARIS

HUNGER AND THIRST

Words and Music by
PHIL MADEIRA

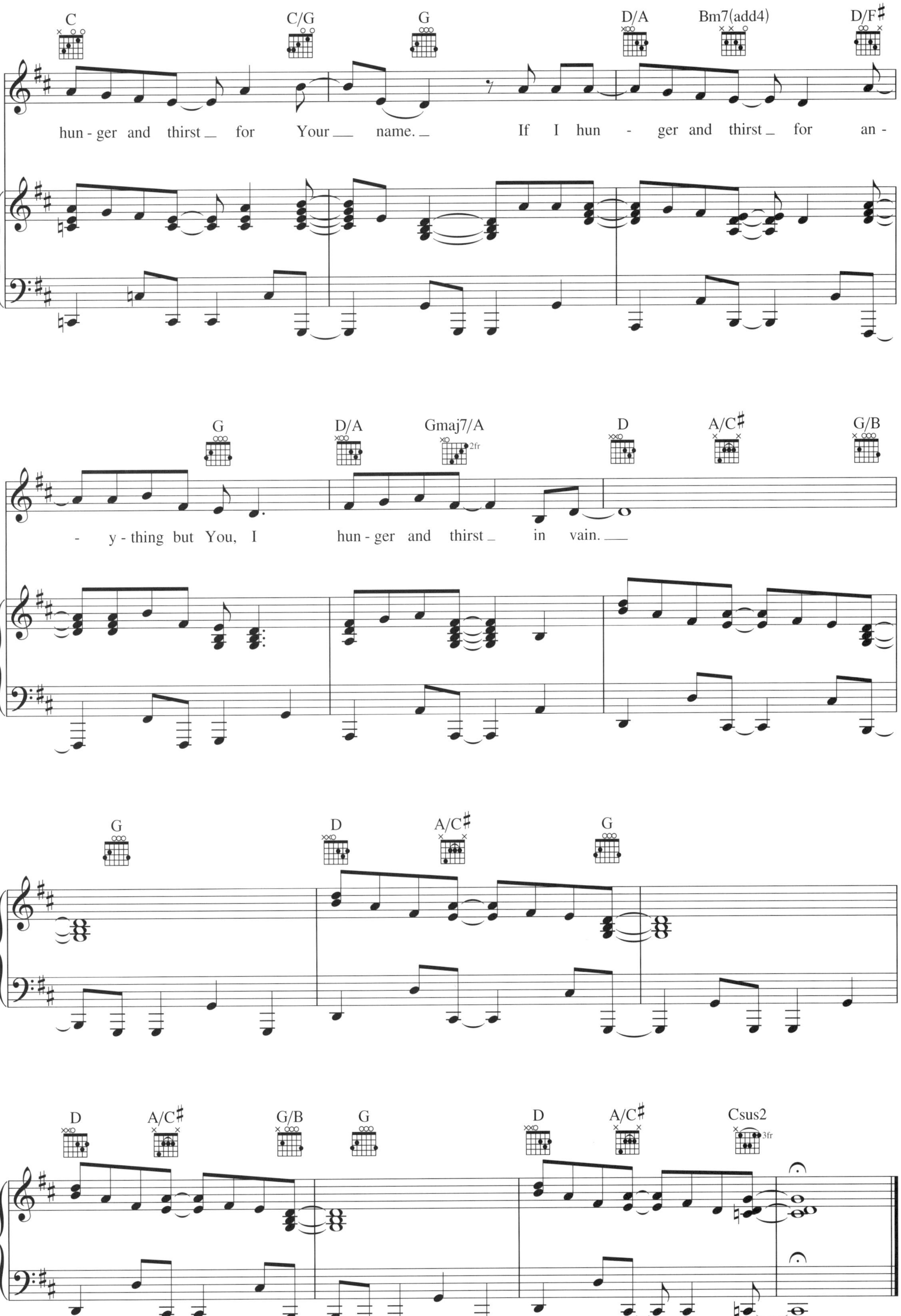
C C/G G D/A Bm7(add4) D/F♯
hun-ger and thirst for Your name. If I hun - ger and thirst for an-
G D/A Gmaj7/A D A/C♯ G/B
- y-thing but You, I hun-ger and thirst in vain.
2fr
G D A/C♯ G
D A/C♯ G/B G D A/C♯ Csus2
3fr

I STILL BELIEVE

Words and Music by
JEREMY CAMP

© 2002 THIRSTY MOON RIVER PUBLISHING (ASCAP) and STOLEN PRIDE MUSIC (ASCAP)
Admin. by EMI CMG PUBLISHING
All Rights Reserved Used by Permission

I WANT TO BE JUST LIKE YOU

Words and Music by JOY BECKER
and DAN DEAN

© 1994 DAWN TREADER MUSIC (SESAC) and PRAISESONG PRESS (ASCAP)
DAWN TREADER MUSIC Admin. by EMI CMG PUBLISHING
All Rights Reserved   Used by Permission

JOY

Words and Music by PETER FURLER
and STEVE TAYLOR

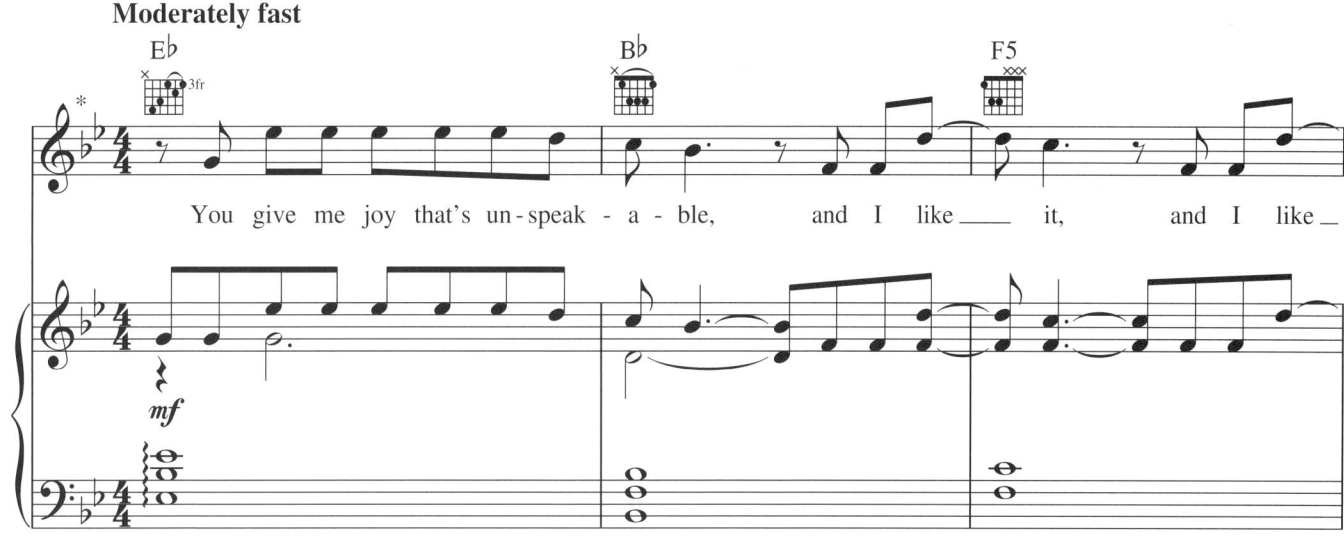

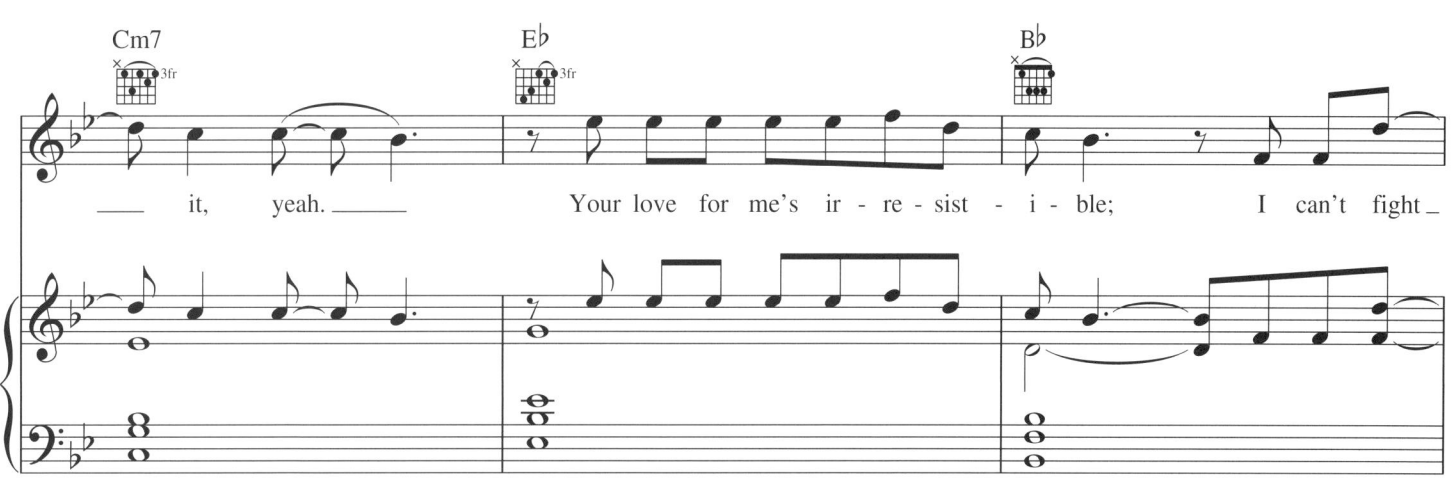

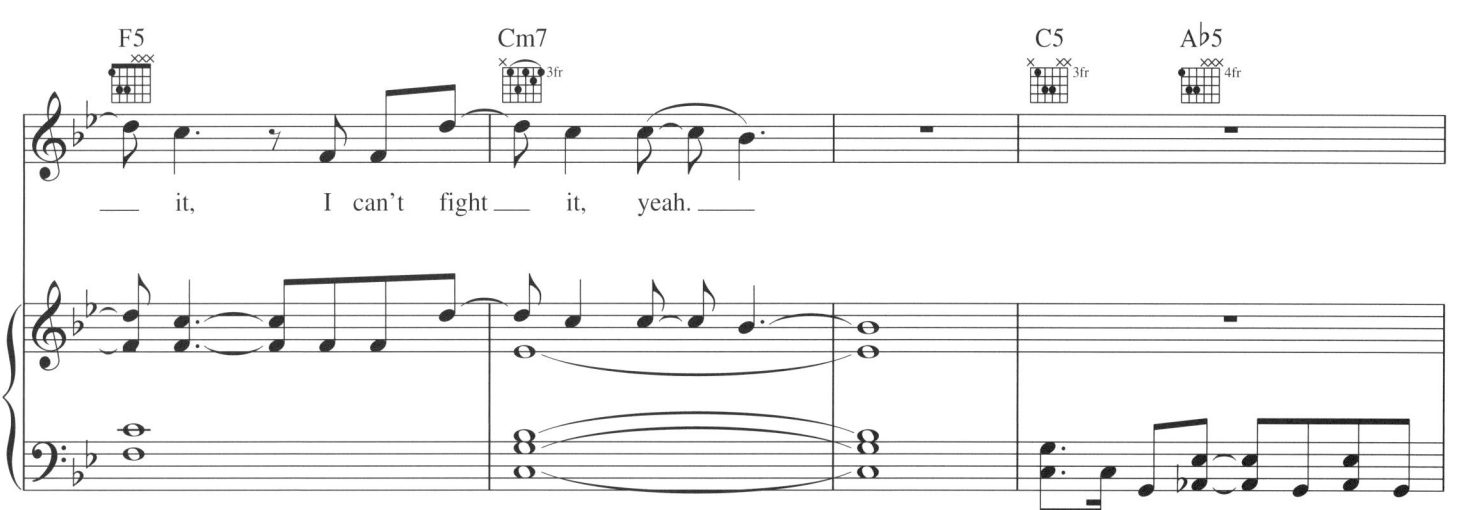

* Recorded a half step higher.

© 2000 DAWN TREADER MUSIC (SESAC) and SOYLENT TUNES (SESAC)
DAWN TREADER MUSIC Admin. by EMI CMG PUBLISHING
SOYLENT TUNES Admin. by ICG
All Rights Reserved   Used by Permission

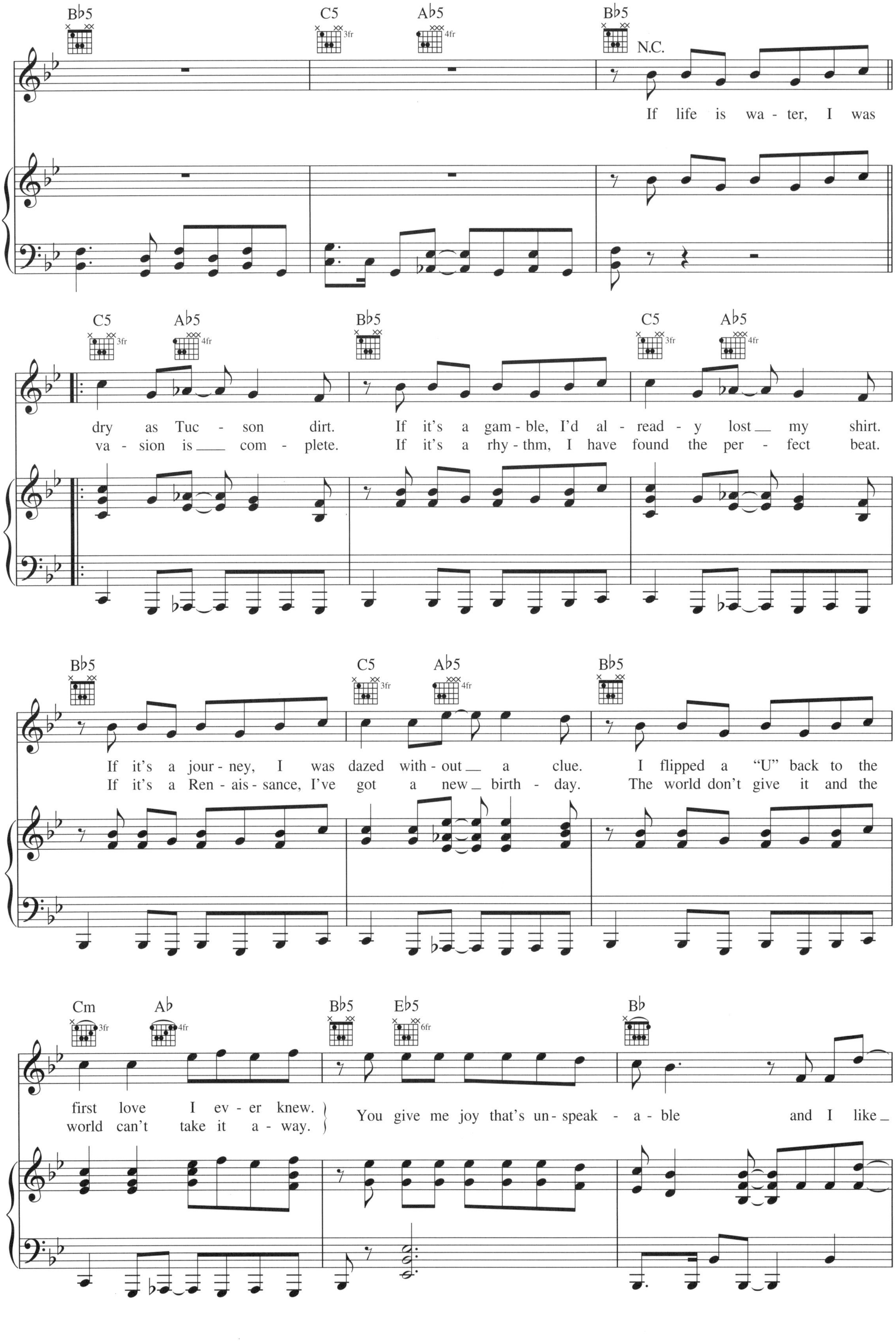
B♭5 C5 A♭5 B♭5
N.C.
If life is wa - ter, I was
C5 A♭5 B♭5 C5 A♭5
dry as Tuc - son dirt. If it's a gam - ble, I'd al - read - y lost my shirt.
va - sion is com - plete. If it's a rhy - thm, I have found the per - fect beat.
B♭5 C5 A♭5 B♭5
If it's a jour - ney, I was dazed with - out a clue. I flipped a "U" back to the
If it's a Ren - ais - sance, I've got a new birth - day. The world don't give it and the
Cm A♭ B♭5 E♭5 B♭
first love I ev - er knew.
world can't take it a - way.
You give me joy that's un - speak - a - ble and I like
3fr
4fr
6fr

146

KNOCKIN' ON HEAVEN'S DOOR

Words and Music by GRANT CUNNINGHAM
and MATT HUESMANN

Lead Me On

Words and Music by MICHAEL W. SMITH,
WAYNE KIRKPATRICK and AMY GRANT

Strong Rock beat

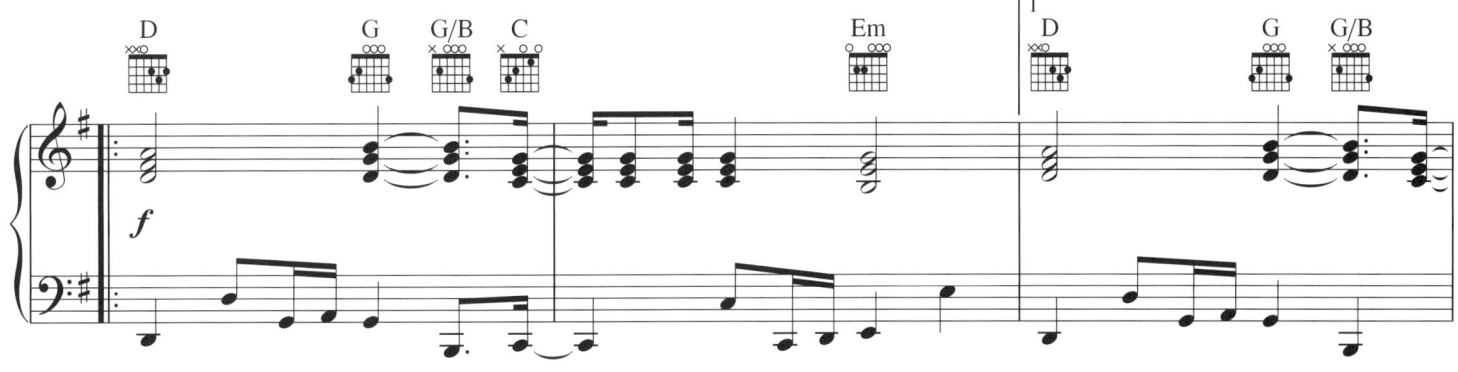
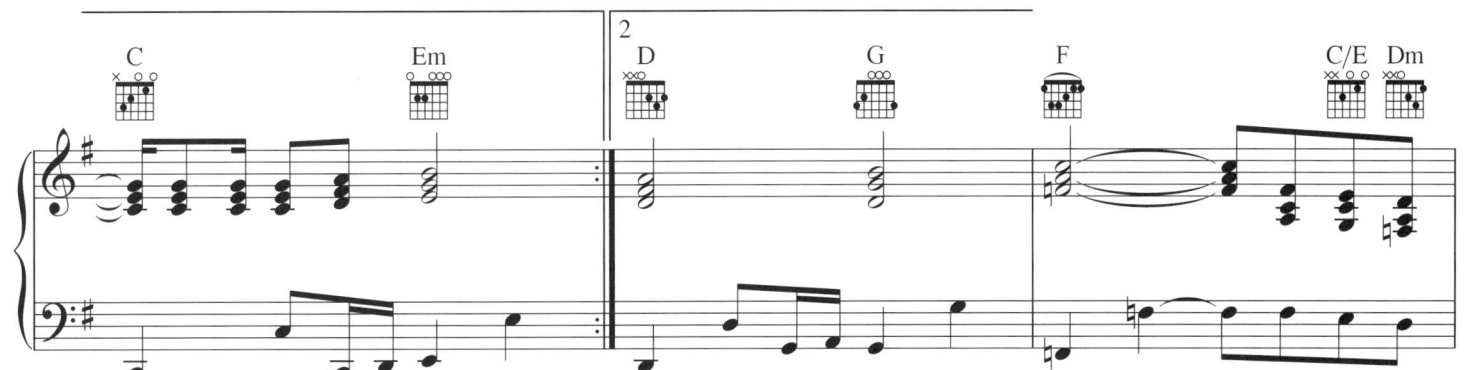

*Recorded a half step lower.

Copyright © 1988 Sony/ATV Music Publishing LLC, Universal Music - Careers and Word Music, LLC
All Rights on behalf of Sony/ATV Music Publishing LLC Administered by Sony/ATV Music Publishing LLC, 8 Music Square West, Nashville, TN 37203
International Copyright Secured   All Rights Reserved

LEGACY

Words and Music by
NICHOLE NORDEMAN

172

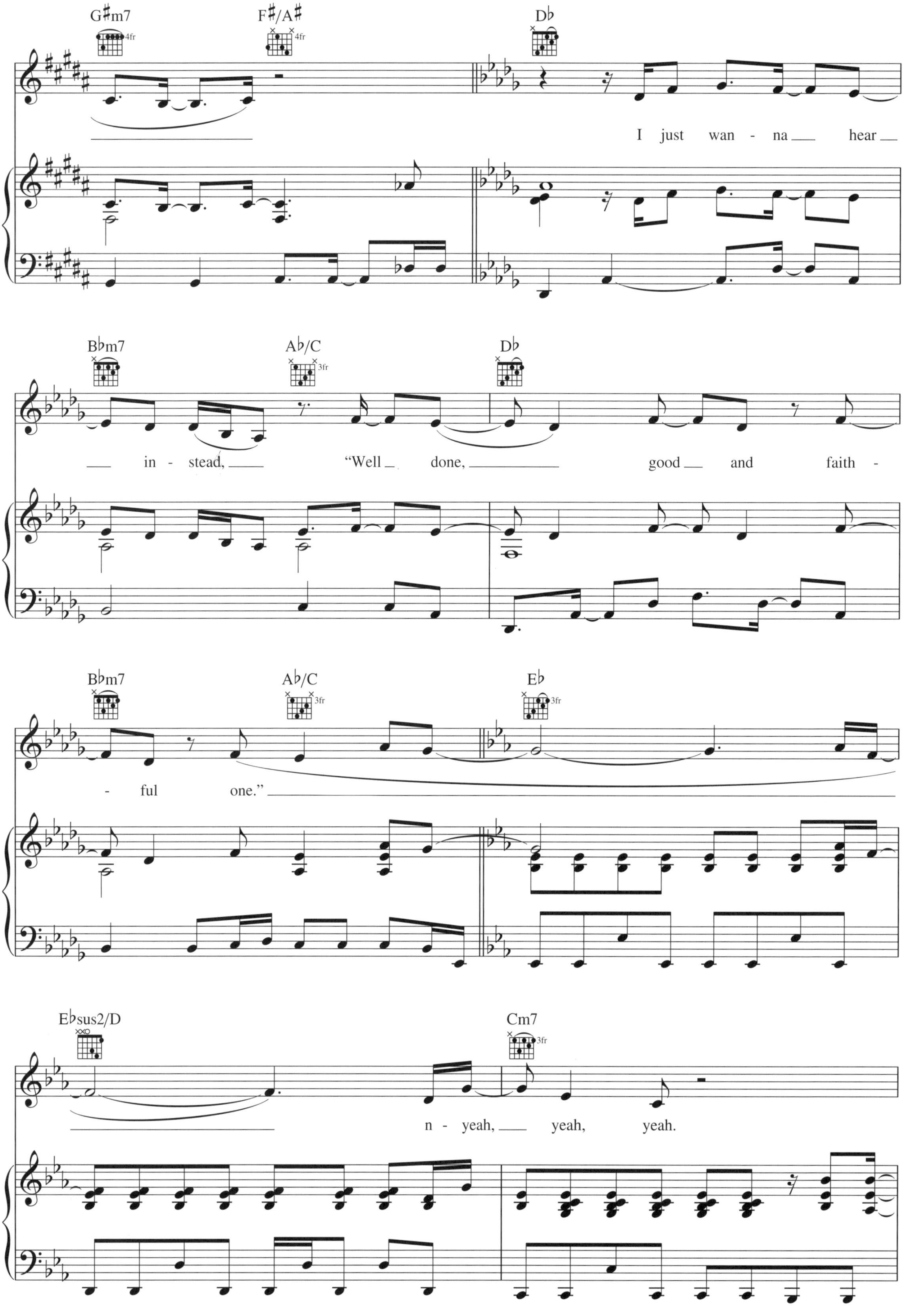
G♯m7
F♯/A♯
D♭
I just wan - na hear
B♭m7
A♭/C
D♭
in - stead, "Well done, good and faith -
B♭m7
A♭/C
E♭
- ful one."
E♭sus2/D
Cm7
n - yeah, yeah, yeah.

LEARNING TO BREATHE

Words and Music by
JONATHAN FOREMAN

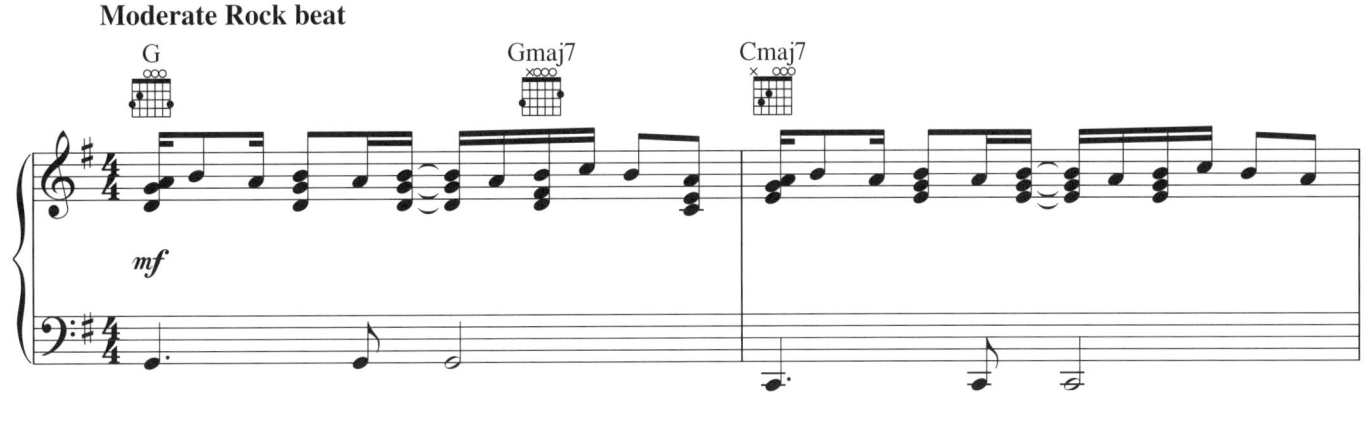
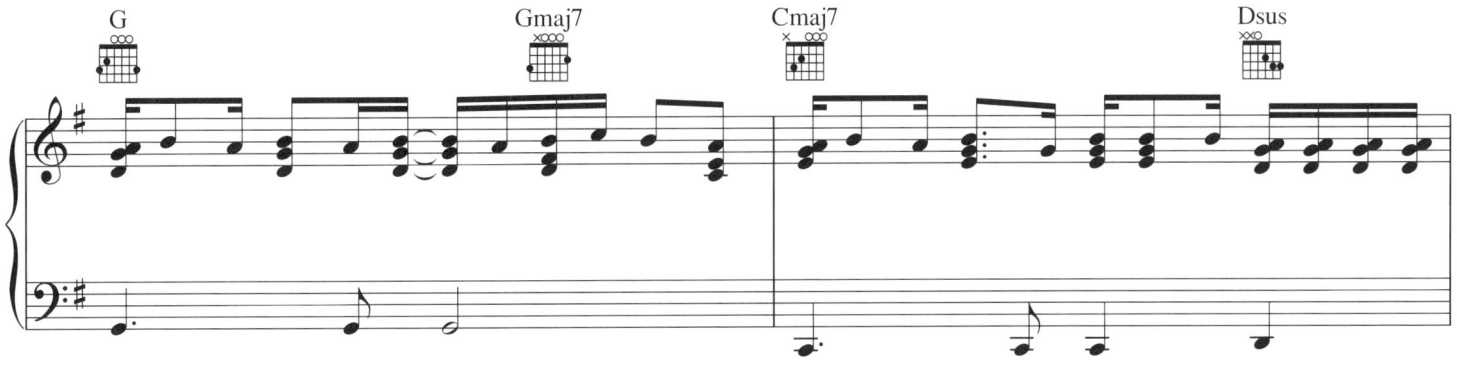
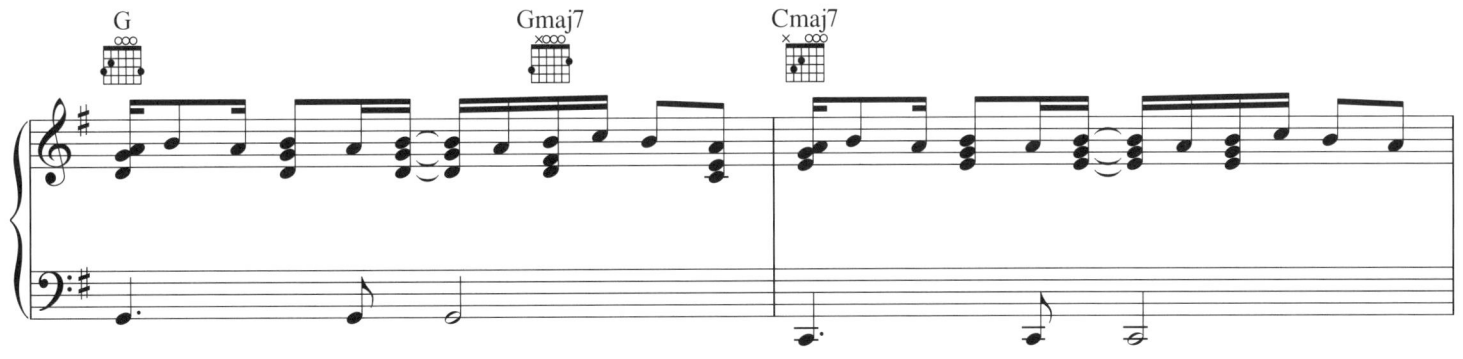
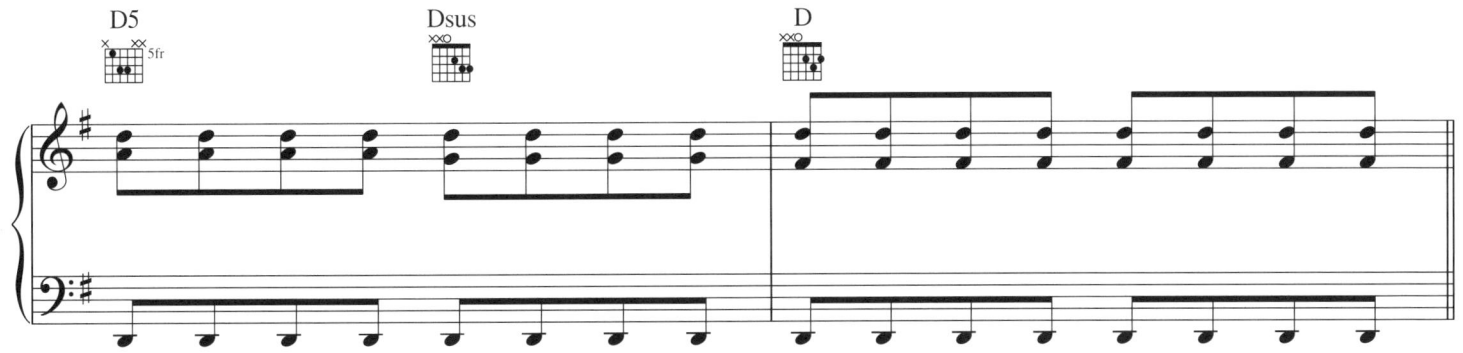

© 2000 MEADOWGREEN MUSIC COMPANY (ASCAP) and SUGAR PETE SONGS (ASCAP)
Admin. by EMI CMG PUBLISHING
All Rights Reserved   Used by Permission

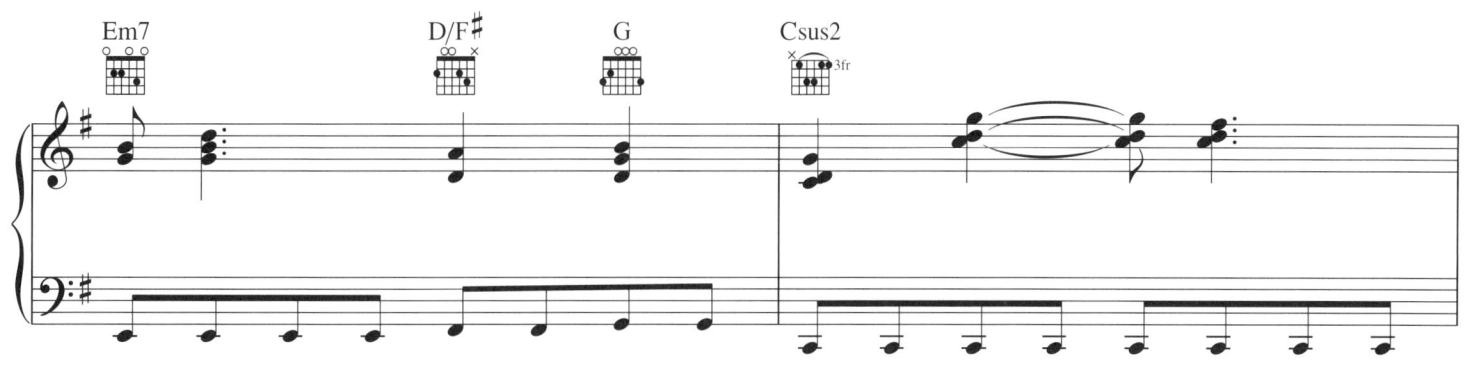
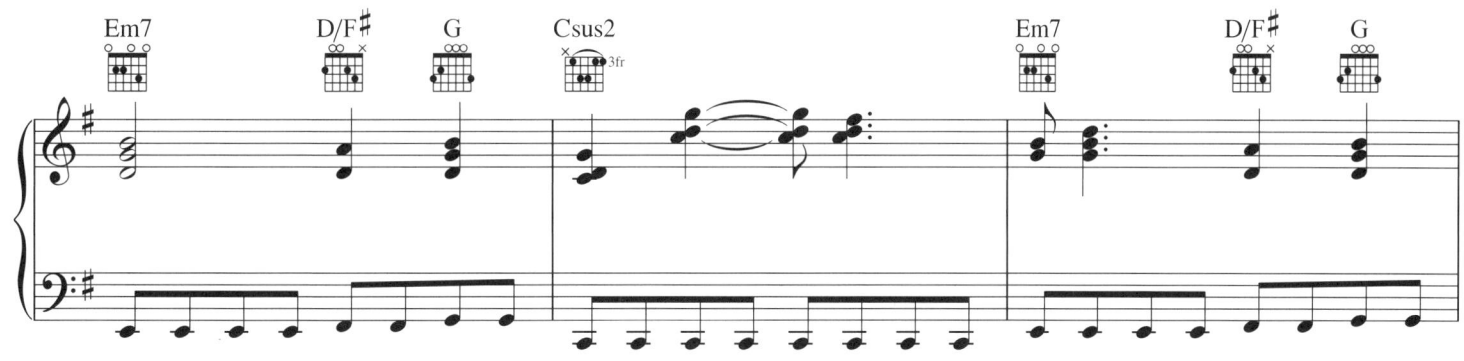
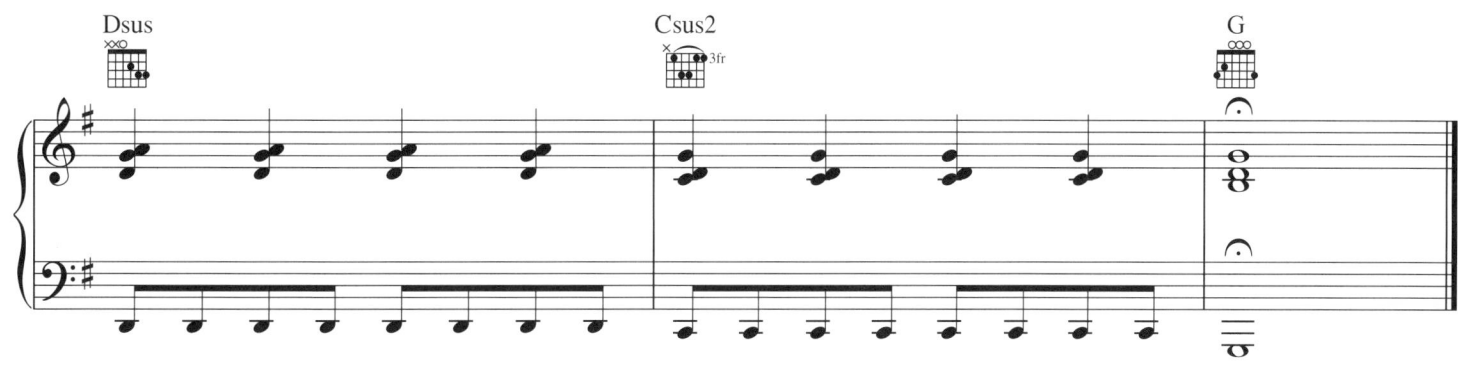

LET IT FADE

Words and Music by JEREMY CAMP
and ADAM WATTS

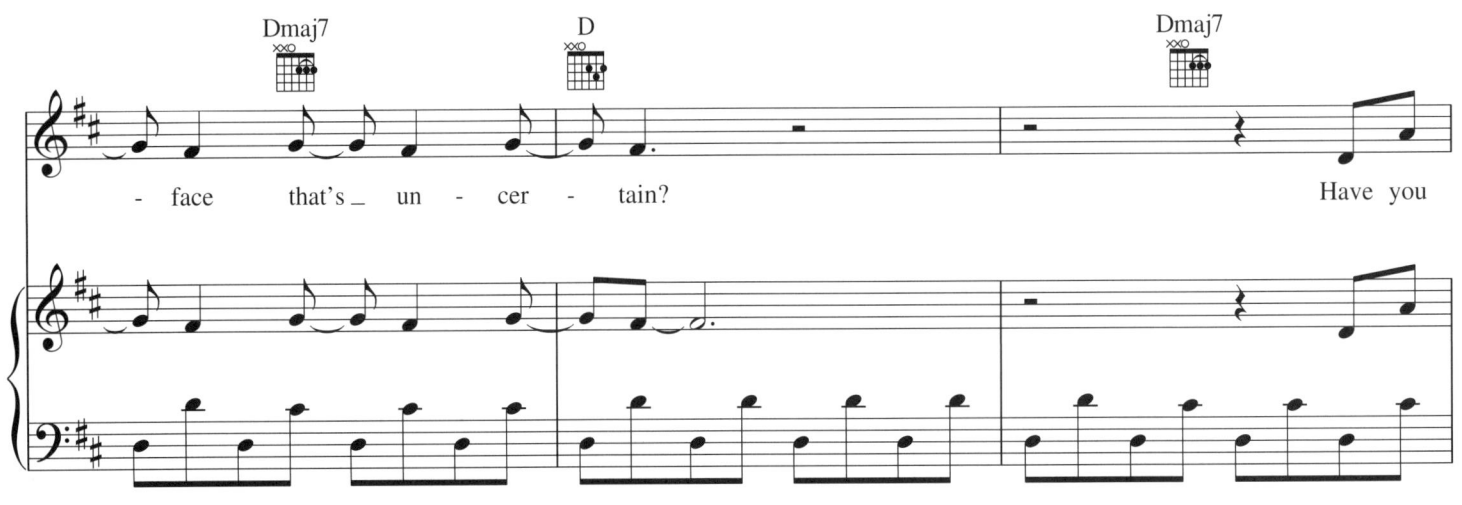

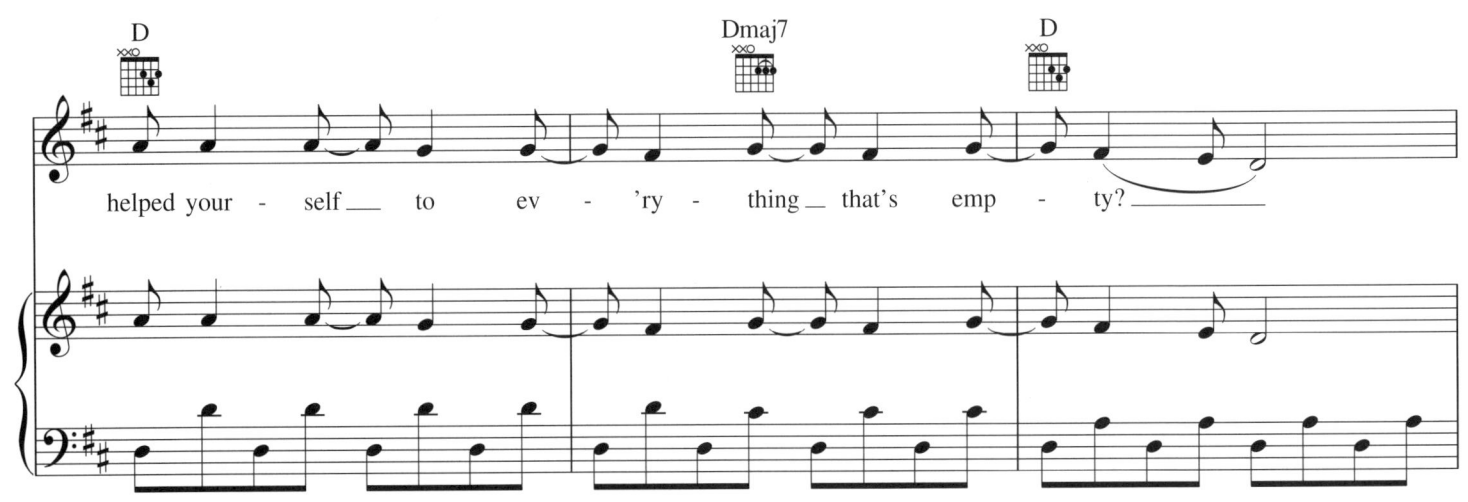

© 2006 THIRSTY MOON RIVER PUBLISHING (ASCAP), STOLEN PRIDE MUSIC (ASCAP), SEVEN PEAKS MUSIC (ASCAP) and DYING EGO MUSIC (ASCAP)
THIRSTY MOON RIVER PUBLISHING and STOLEN PRIDE MUSIC Admin. by EMI CMG PUBLISHING
DYING EGO MUSIC Admin. by SEVEN PEAKS MUSIC
All Rights Reserved Used by Permission

LET US PRAY

Words and Music by
STEVEN CURTIS CHAPMAN

LOSE MY SOUL

Words and Music by TOBY McKEEHAN,
MICHAEL RIPOLL and CHRIS STEPHENS

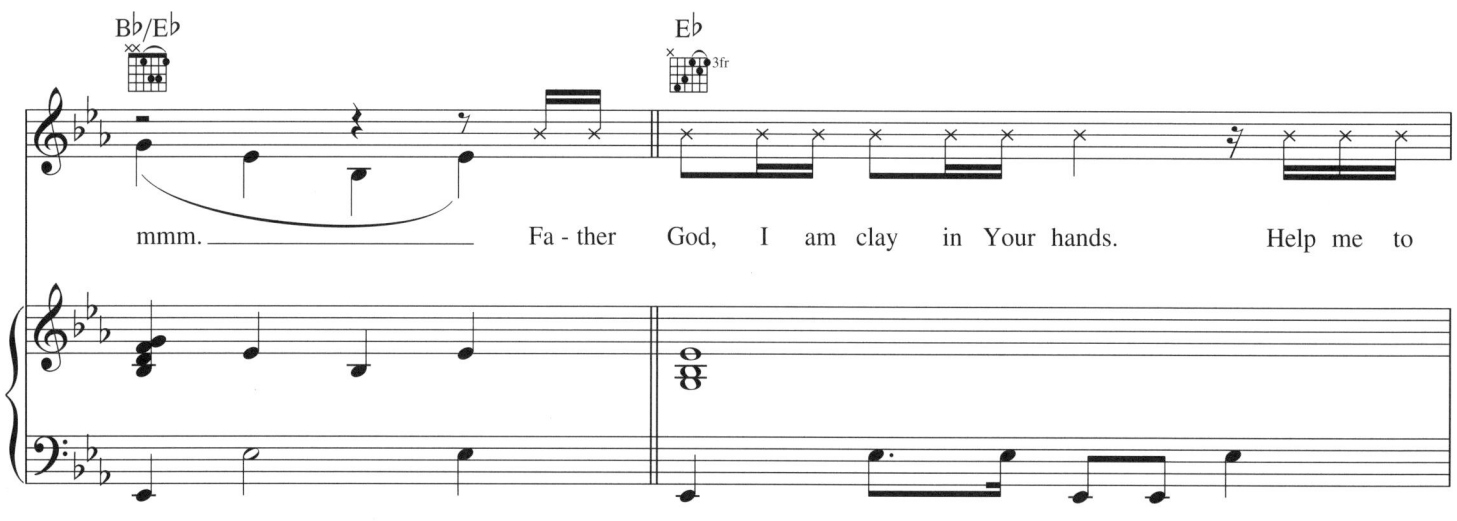

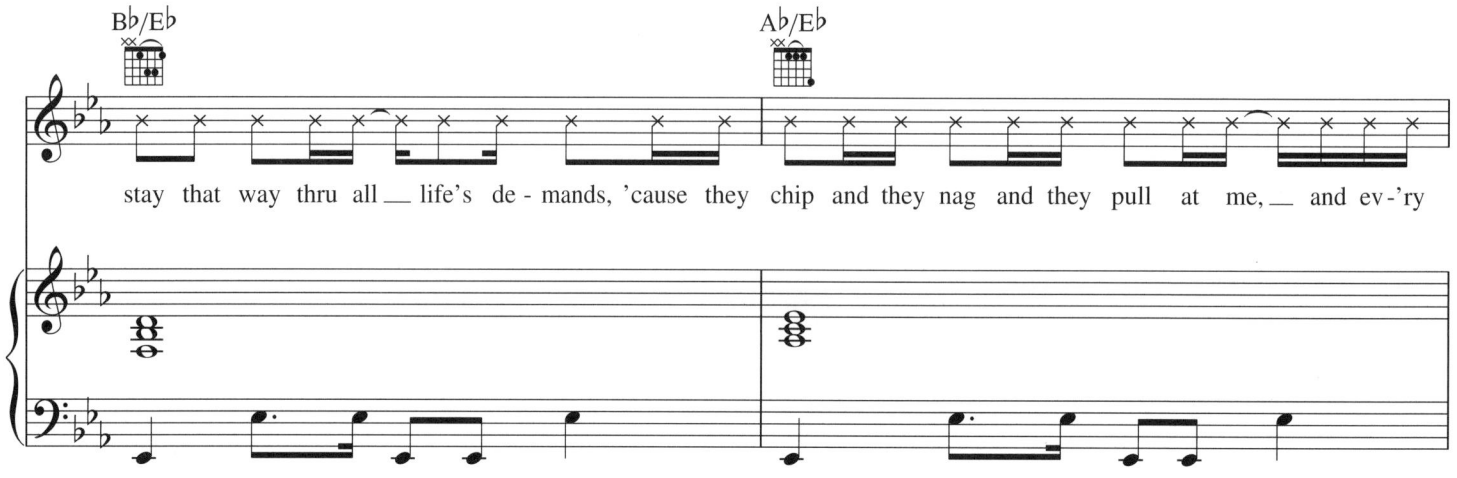

© 2007 GOTEE MUSIC (BMI), REGISFUNK MUSIC (BMI), ACHTOBER SONGS (BMI) and FUNK IN YA JAZZ PUBLISHING (ASCAP)
GOTEE MUSIC, REGISFUNK MUSIC and ACHTOBER SONGS Admin. by EMI CMG PUBLISHING
FUNK IN YA JAZZ PUBLISHING Admin. by THE COPYRIGHT COMPANY, Nashville, TN
All Rights Reserved   Used by Permission

225

NO BETTER PLACE

Words and Music by STEVEN CURTIS CHAPMAN
and PHIL NAISH

*Recorded a half step higher.

© 1990 SPARROW SONG (BMI), GREG NELSON MUSIC (BMI), DAVAUB MUSIC (ASCAP) and UNIVERSAL MUSIC - CAREERS (BMI)
SPARROW SONG, GREG NELSON MUSIC and DAVAUB MUSIC Admin. by EMI CMG PUBLISHING
All Rights Reserved   Used by Permission

NOTHING COMPARES

Words and Music by MAC POWELL, MARK LEE, BRAD AVERY, TAI ANDERSON and DAVID CARR

© 2001 VANDURA 2500 SONGS (ASCAP) and NEW SPRING PUBLISHING, INC. (ASCAP)
VANDURA 2500 SONGS Admin. by EMI CMG PUBLISHING
NEW SPRING PUBLISHING, INC. Admin. by BRENTWOOD-BENSON MUSIC PUBLISHING, INC.
All Rights Reserved Used by Permission

Additional Spoken Lyrics

*And those words that were spoken and written by the apostle Paul apply just as much
To our lives today as they did two thousand years ago when he wrote them.
That in our lives, no matter where we could go, or who we could meet,
Or what we could see, or what we could earn, or be given to us, or accomplish,
There is nothing in our lives that will ever even come close to the greatness of knowing Jesus Christ our Lord.*

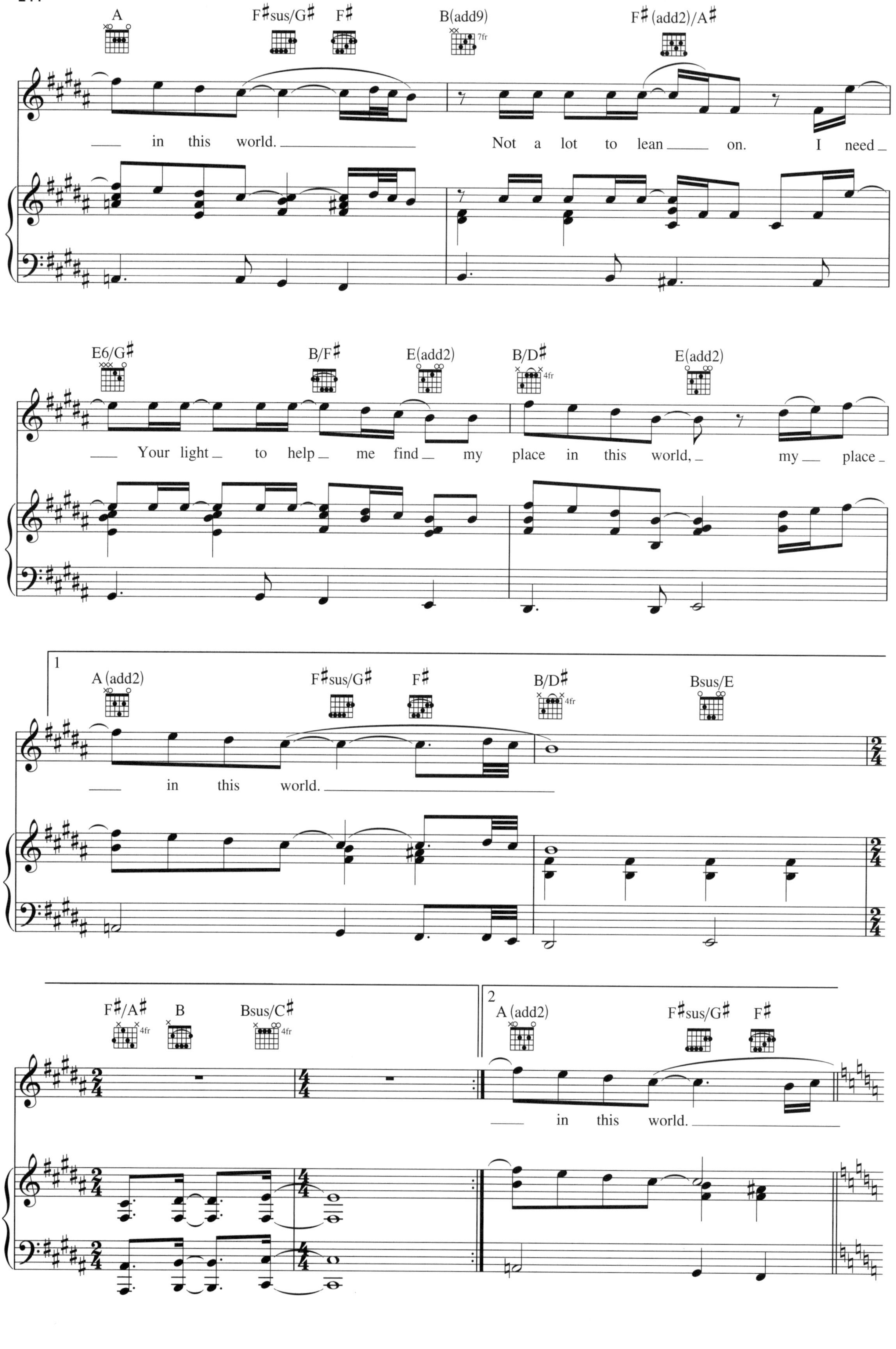
A
F♯sus/G♯
F♯
B(add9)
7fr
F♯(add2)/A♯
in this world.
Not a lot to lean on. I need
E6/G♯
B/F♯
E(add2)
B/D♯
4fr
E(add2)
Your light to help me find my place in this world, my place
1
A(add2)
F♯sus/G♯
F♯
B/D♯
4fr
Bsus/E
in this world.
F♯/A♯
4fr
B
Bsus/C♯
4fr
2
A(add2)
F♯sus/G♯
F♯
in this world.

Praise You In This Storm

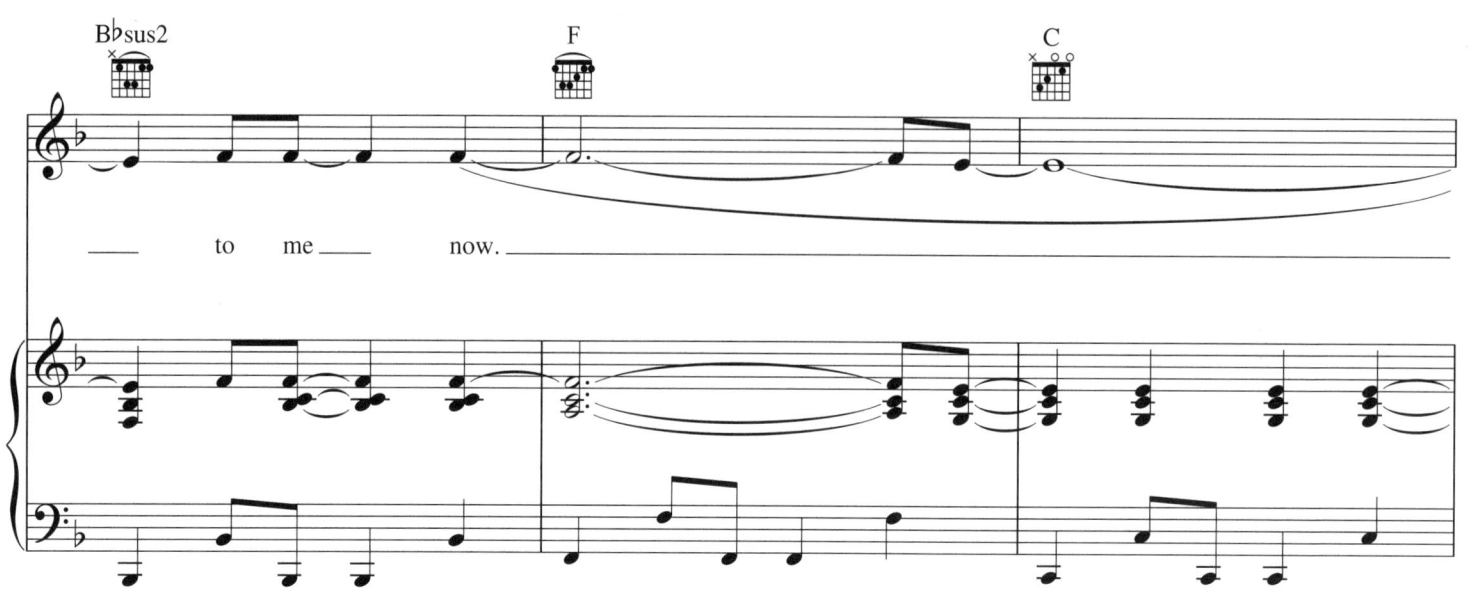

REVOLUTIONARY LOVE

Words and Music by DAVID CROWDER, JACK PARKER and JEREMY BUSH

© 2003 WORSHIPTOGETHER.COM SONGS (ASCAP), sixsteps Music (ASCAP) and INOT MUSIC (ASCAP)
Admin. by EMI CMG PUBLISHING
All Rights Reserved Used by Permission

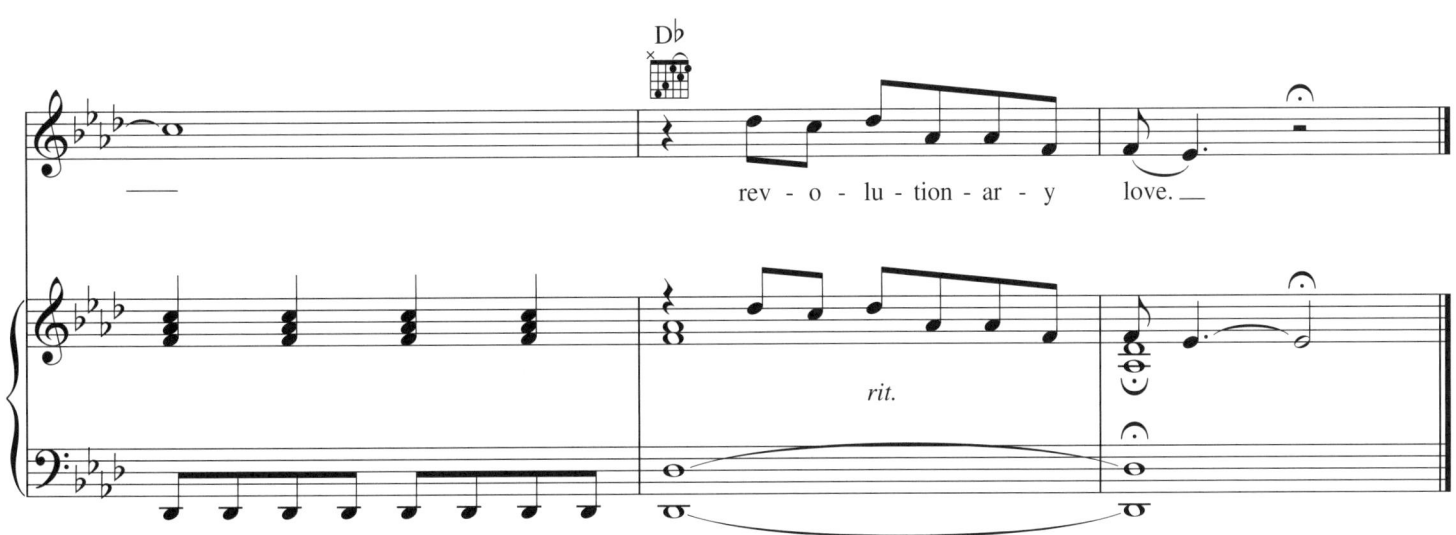

SAVING GRACE

Words and Music by GRANT CUNNINGHAM
and MATT HUESMANN

© 1998 IMAGINE THIS (BMI), RIVER OAKS MUSIC COMPANY (BMI) and MATT HUESMANN MUSIC (ASCAP)
IMAGINE THIS and RIVER OAKS MUSIC COMPANY Admin. by EMI CMG PUBLISHING
MATT HUESMANN MUSIC Admin. by BUG MUSIC
All Rights Reserved Used by Permission

SING A SONG

Words and Music by MAC POWELL,
MARK LEE, BRAD AVERY,
TAI ANDERSON and DAVID CARR

© 2003 CONSUMING FIRE MUSIC (ASCAP)
Admin. by EMI CMG PUBLISHING
All Rights Reserved   Used by Permission

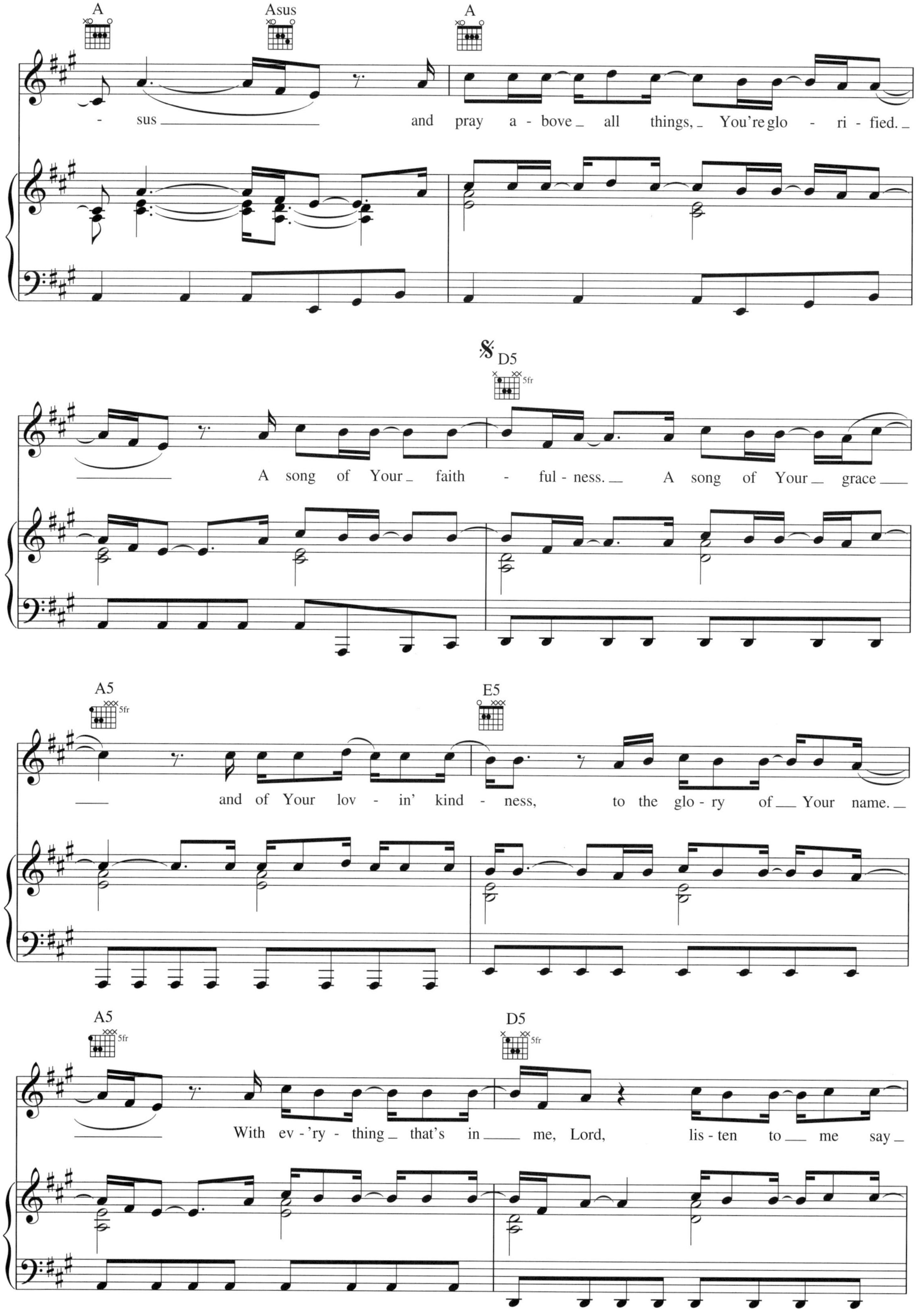
A
Asus
A
- sus and pray a - bove all things, You're glo - ri - fied.
D5
5fr
A song of Your faith - ful - ness. A song of Your grace
A5
5fr
E5
and of Your lov - in' kind - ness, to the glo - ry of Your name.
A5
5fr
D5
5fr
With ev - 'ry - thing that's in me, Lord, lis - ten to me say

SEA OF FACES

Words and Music by JON MICAH SUMRALL,
KYLE MITCHELL, JAMES MEAD,
RYAN SHROUT and AARON SPRINKLE

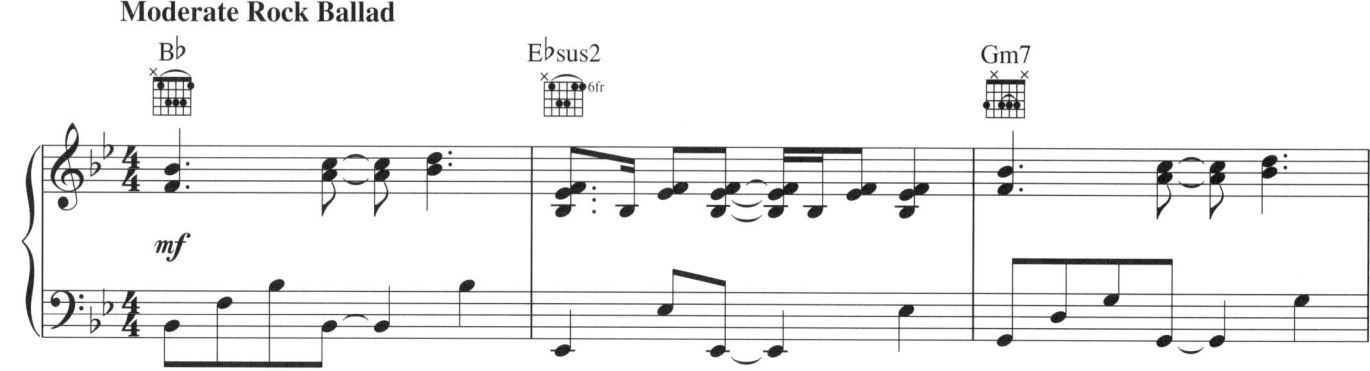
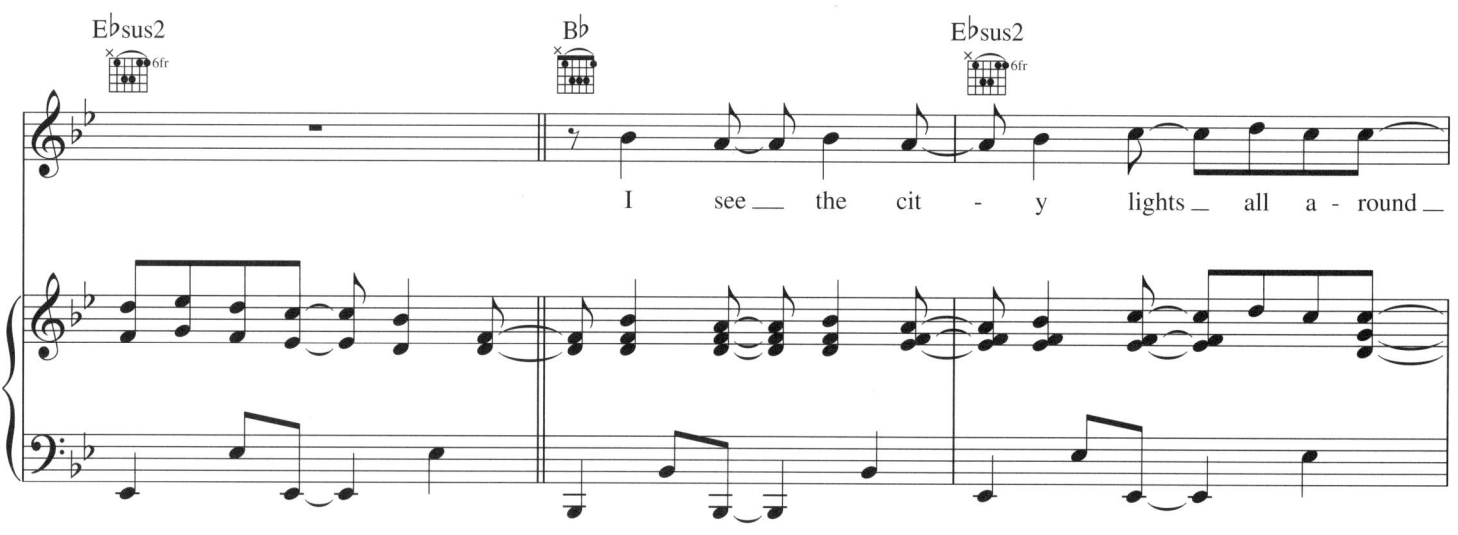

© 2004 THIRSTY MOON RIVER PUBLISHING, INC. (ASCAP), INDECISIVE MUSIC PUBLISHING (ASCAP), Spinning Audio Vortex, Inc. (BMI) and SOLID PEOPLE SONGS (BMI)
Admin. by EMI CMG PUBLISHING
All Rights Reserved Used by Permission

SHINE

Words and Music by PETER FURLER
and STEVE TAYLOR

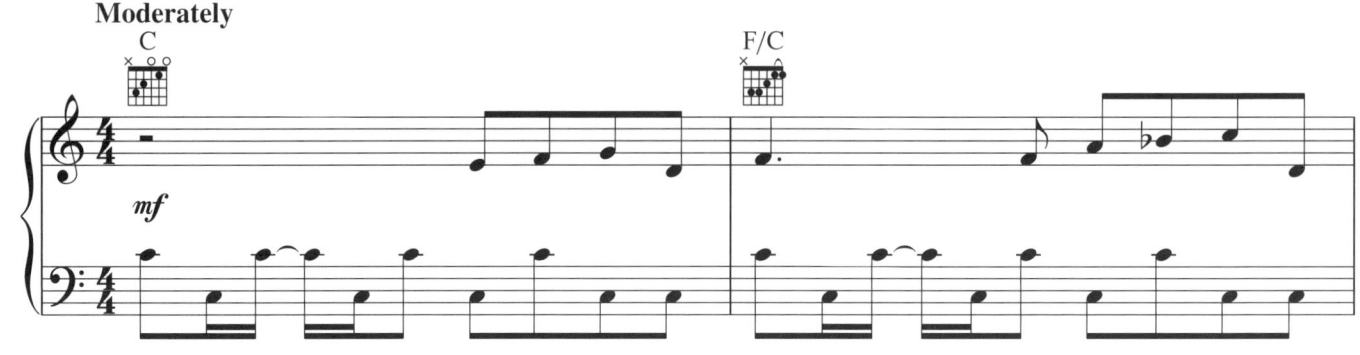

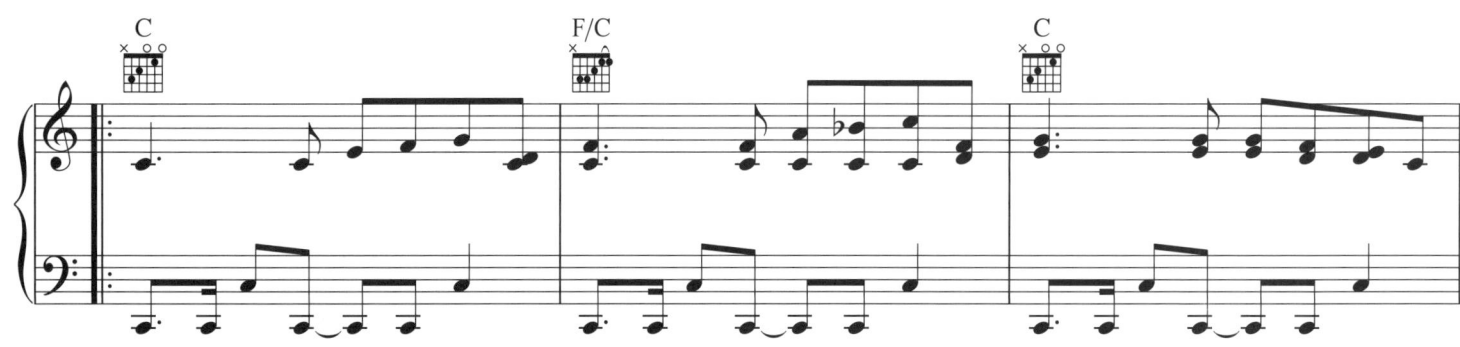
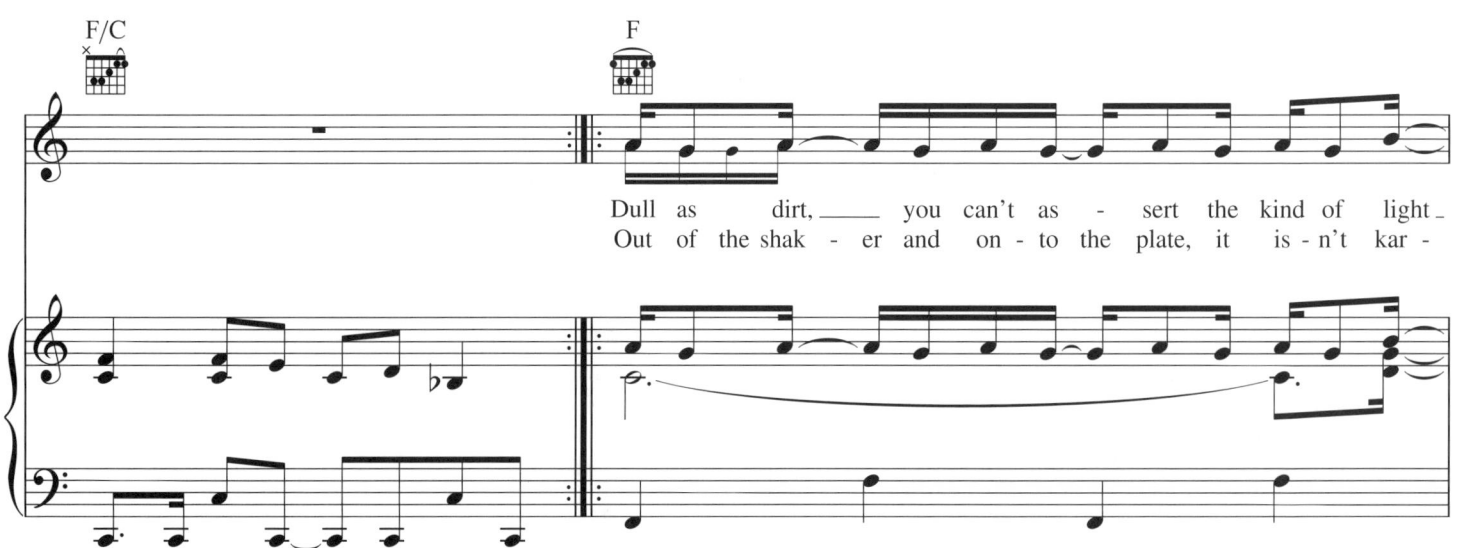

Dull as dirt,____ you can't as-sert the kind of light____
Out of the shak-er and on-to the plate, it is-n't kar-

© 1994 ARIOSE MUSIC (ASCAP), SOYLENT TUNES (SESAC) and SOJOURNER MUSIC (SESAC)
ARIOSE MUSIC Admin. by EMI CMG PUBLISHING
SOYLENT TUNES Admin. by ICG
SOJOURNER MUSIC Admin. by WORDSPRING MUSIC, LLC
All Rights Reserved   Used by Permission

SOMETIMES BY STEP

Words and Music by
DAVID "BEAKER" STRASSER

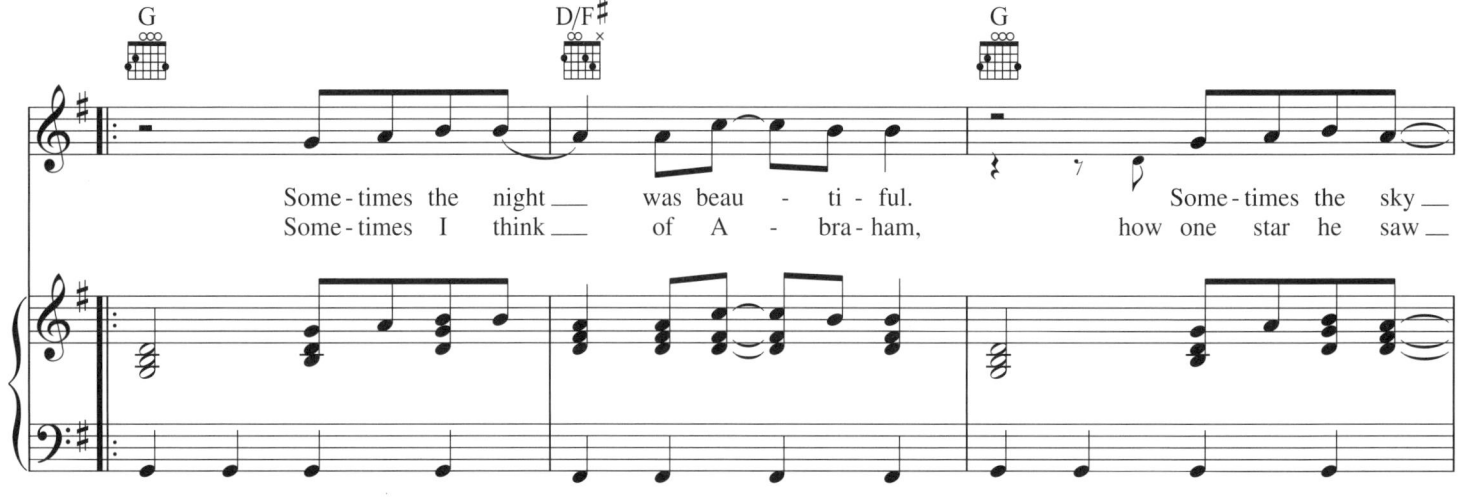
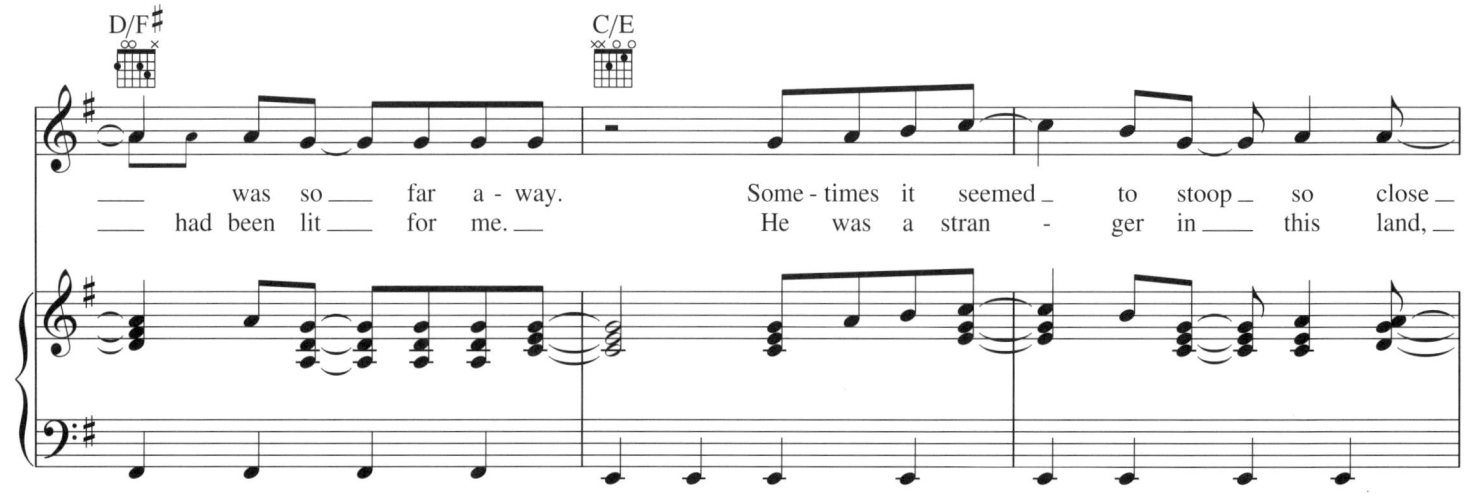

Copyright © 1992 by Universal - MGB Songs and Kid Brothers Of St. Frank Publishing
All Rights Administered by Universal - MGB Songs
International Copyright Secured   All Rights Reserved

SONG OF LOVE

Words and Music by REBECCA ST. JAMES,
MATT BRONLEEWE and JEREMY ASH

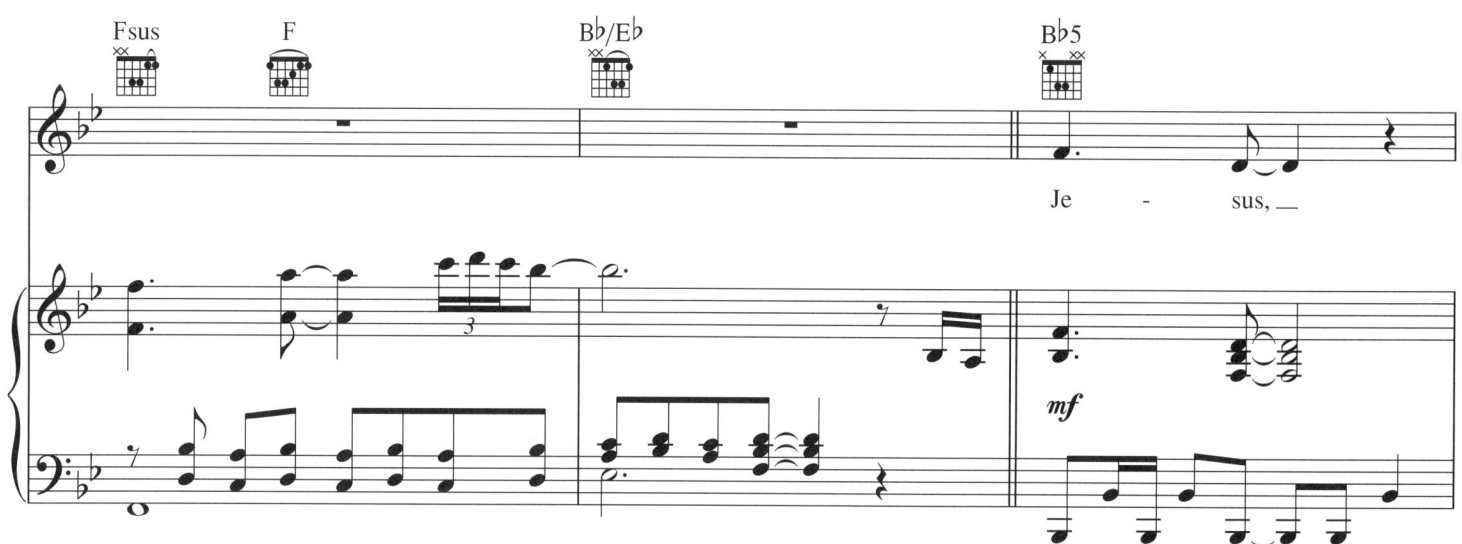

*Recorded a half step higher.

© 2002 UP IN THE MIX MUSIC (BMI), BIBBITSONG MUSIC (BMI), BUG MUSIC-SONGS OF WINDSWEPT PACIFIC (BMI), SONGS FROM THE FARM (BMI),
BUG MUSIC-MUSIC OF WINDSWEPT (ASCAP), GRANGE ROAD MUSIC (ASCAP), TYPICAL HITS (ASCAP) and PROJECT 76 MUSIC (ASCAP)
UP IN THE MIX MUSIC and BIBBITSONG MUSIC Admin. by EMI CMG PUBLISHING
GRANGE ROAD MUSIC, TYPICAL HITS and PROJECT 76 MUSIC Admin. by BUG MUSIC-MUSIC OF WINDSWEPT
SONGS FROM THE FARM Admin. by BUG MUSIC-SONGS OF WINDSWEPT PACIFIC
All Rights Reserved   Used by Permission

SPOKEN FOR

Words and Music by BART MILLARD,
JIM BRYSON, MIKE SCHEUCHZER,
NATHAN COCHRAN, ROBBY SHAFFER
and PETE KIPLEY

Take this world from me;
I don't need it anymore.
Now I have a peace
that I've never known before.

© 2002 Simpleville Music (ASCAP), Wordspring Music, LLC (SESAC) and Songs From The Indigo Room (SESAC)
All Rights for Simpleville Music Administered by Simpleville Music, Inc.
All Rights for Songs From The Indigo Room Administered by Wordspring Music, LLC
All Rights Reserved   Used by Permission

THIS IS YOUR LIFE

Words and Music by
JONATHAN FOREMAN

Moderately slow, in 2

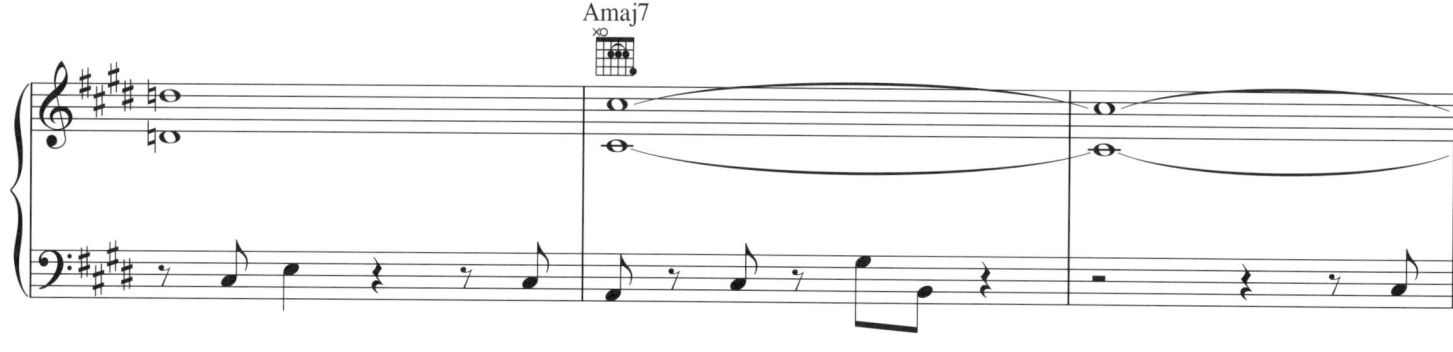

© 2003 MEADOWGREEN MUSIC COMPANY (ASCAP) and SUGAR PETE SONGS (ASCAP)
Admin. by EMI CMG PUBLISHING
All Rights Reserved   Used by Permission

UNDO

Words and Music by SCOTT DAVIS, WES WILLIS and KEVIN HUGULEY

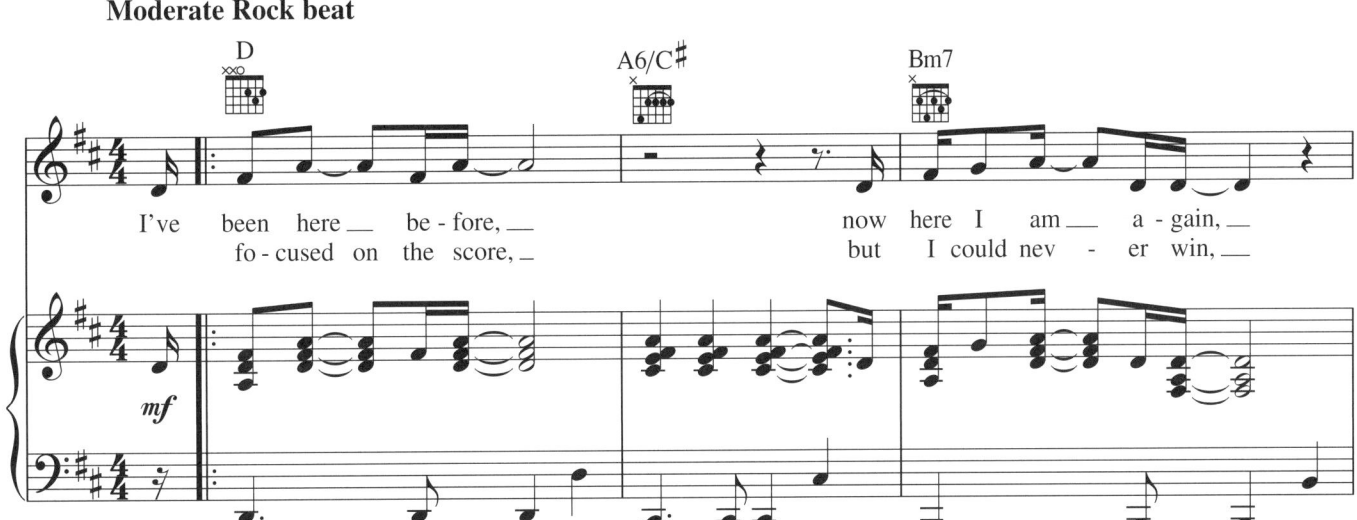

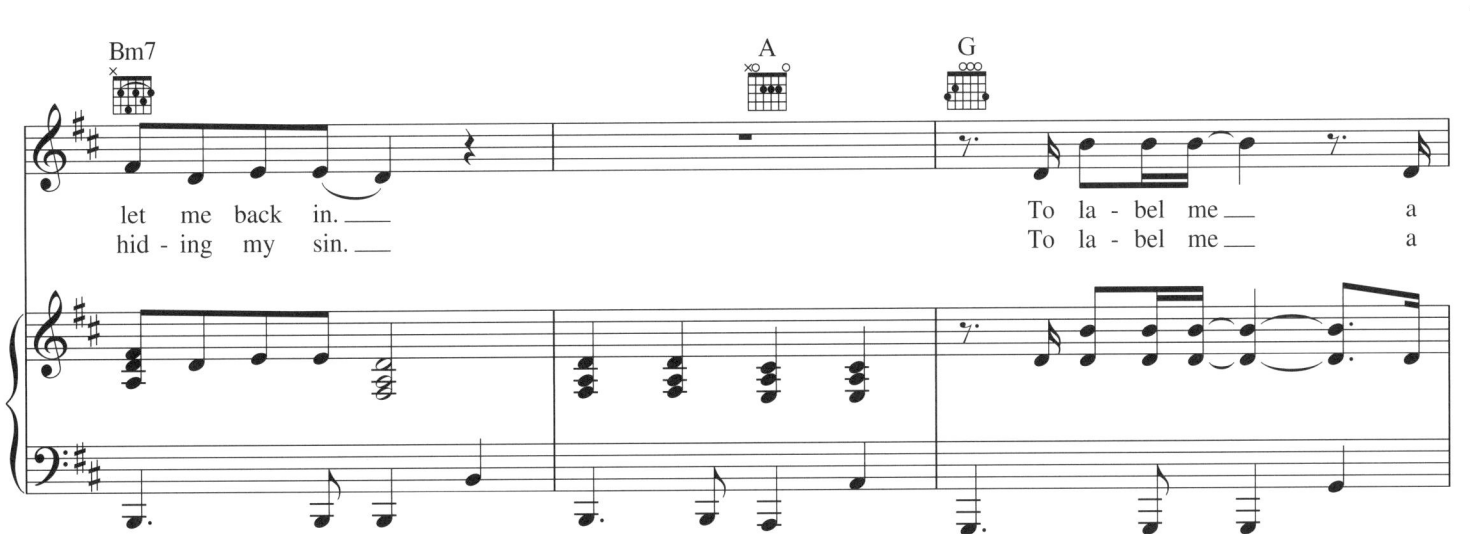

© 2007 MEAUX HITS (ASCAP) and MIDAS MAGIC (ASCAP)
MEAUX HITS Admin. by EMI CMG PUBLISHING
All Rights Reserved   Used by Permission

that You turn me a-round, pick me up, un-do what I've be-come. Bring me back to the place of for-give-ness and grace. I need You, I need Your help; I can't do this my-self. You're the on-ly One who can

THIS MAN

Words and Music by
JEREMY CAMP

WE NEED JESUS

By JOHN ELEFANTE, DINO ELEFANTE and SCOTT SPRINGER

WONDER WHY

Words and Music by GRANT CUNNINGHAM
and MATT HUESMANN

© 2001 IMAGINE THIS MUSIC (ASCAP), MEADOWGREEN MUSIC COMPANY (ASCAP) and MATT HUESMANN MUSIC (ASCAP)
IMAGINE THIS MUSIC and MEADOWGREEN MUSIC COMPANY Admin. by EMI CMG PUBLISHING
MATT HUESMANN MUSIC Admin. by BUG MUSIC
All Rights Reserved   Used by Permission

WHAT IF I STUMBLE

Words and Music by TOBY McKEEHAN and DANIEL JOSEPH

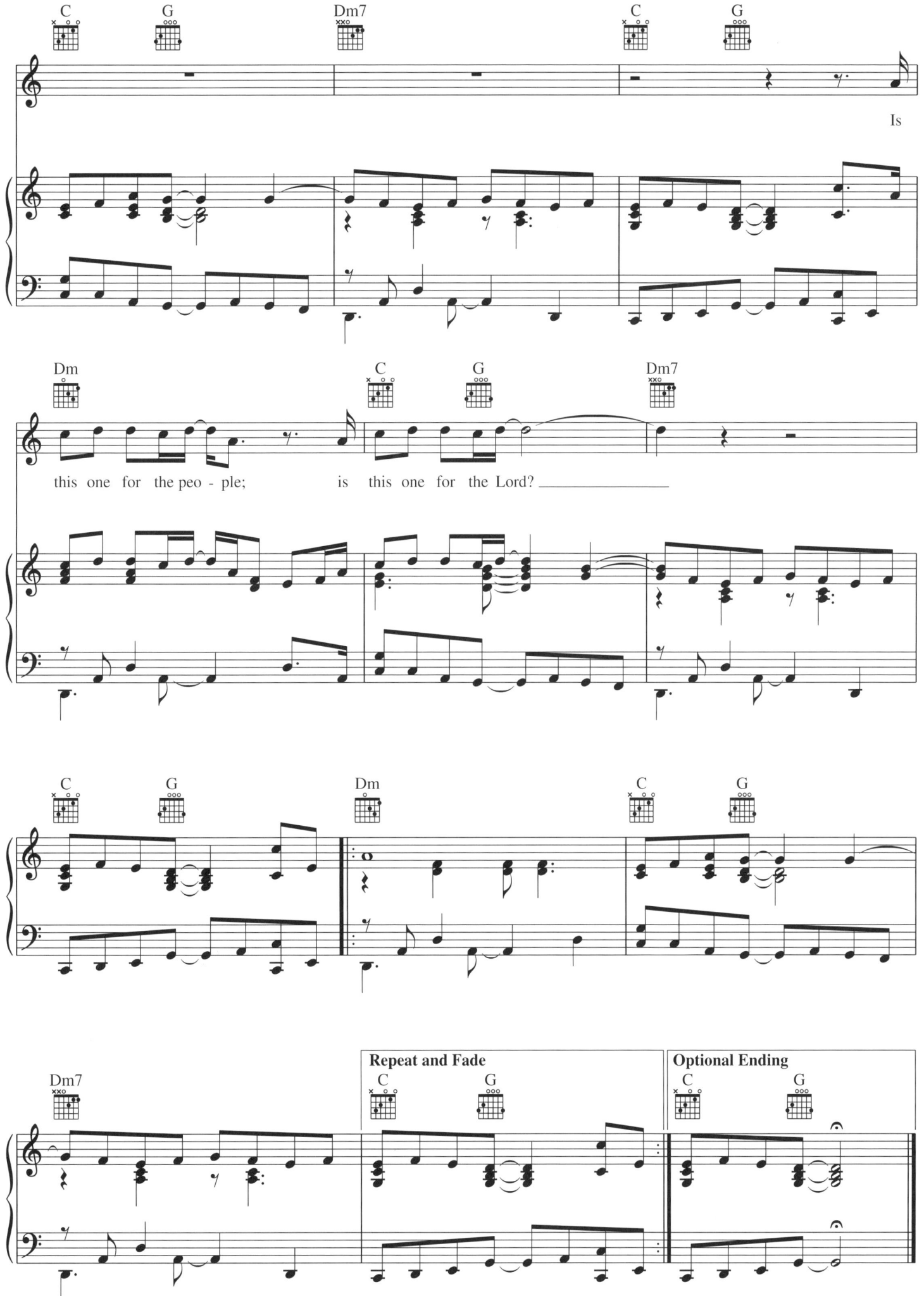

Whatever You're Doing
(Something Heavenly)

Words and Music by MATT HAMMITT,
CHRIS ROHMAN, MARK GRAALMAN,
DAN GARTLEY and PETER PROVOST

© 2008 BIRDWING MUSIC (ASCAP)
Admin. by EMI CMG PUBLISHING
All Rights Reserved Used by Permission

YOU ARE THE ANSWER

Words and Music by MATT HUESMANN
and REGIE HAMM

HAL•LEONARD ESSENTIAL SONGS

Play the best songs from the Roaring '20s to today! Each collection features dozens of the most memorable songs of each decade, or in your favorite musical style, arranged in piano/vocal/guitar format.

THE 1920s
Over 100 songs that shaped the decade: Ain't We Got Fun? • Basin Street Blues • Bye Bye Blackbird • Can't Help Lovin' Dat Man • I Wanna Be Loved by You • Makin' Whoopee • Ol' Man River • Puttin' On the Ritz • Toot, Toot, Tootsie • Yes Sir, That's My Baby • and more.
00311200 .... $24.95

THE 1930s
97 essential songs from the 1930s: April in Paris • Body and Soul • Cheek to Cheek • Falling in Love with Love • Georgia on My Mind • Heart and Soul • I'll Be Seeing You • The Lady Is a Tramp • Mood Indigo • My Funny Valentine • You Are My Sunshine • and more.
00311193 .... $24.95

THE 1940s
An amazing collection of over 100 songs from the '40s: Boogie Woogie Bugle Boy • Don't Get Around Much Anymore • Have I Told You Lately That I Love You • I'll Remember April • Route 66 • Sentimental Journey • Take the "A" Train • You'd Be So Nice to Come Home To • and more.
00311192 .... $24.95

THE 1950s
Over 100 pivotal songs from the 1950s, including: All Shook Up • Bye Bye Love • Chantilly Lace • Fever • Great Balls of Fire • Kansas City • Love and Marriage • Mister Sandman • Rock Around the Clock • Sixteen Tons • Tennessee Waltz • Wonderful! Wonderful! • and more.
00311191 .... $24.95

THE 1960s
104 '60s essentials, including: Baby Love • California Girls • Dancing in the Street • Hey Jude • I Heard It Through the Grapevine • Respect • Stand by Me • Twist and Shout • Will You Love Me Tomorrow • Yesterday • You Keep Me Hangin' On • and more.
00311190 .... $24.95

THE 1970s
Over 80 of the best songs from the '70s: American Pie • Band on the Run • Come Sail Away • Dust in the Wind • I Feel the Earth Move • Let It Be • Morning Has Broken • Smoke on the Water • Take a Chance on Me • The Way We Were • You're So Vain • and more.
00311189 .... $24.95

THE 1980s
Over 70 classics from the age of power pop and hair metal: Against All Odds • Call Me • Ebony and Ivory • The Heat Is On • Jump • Manic Monday • Sister Christian • Time After Time • Up Where We Belong • What's Love Got to Do with It • and more.
00311188 .... $24.95

Complete contents listings are available online at

Prices, contents and availability subject to change without notice.

THE 1990s
68 songs featuring country-crossover, swing revival, the birth of grunge, and more: Change the World • Fields of Gold • Ironic • Livin' La Vida Loca • More Than Words • Smells like Teen Spirit • Walking in Memphis • Zoot Suit Riot • and more.
00311187 .... $24.95

THE 2000s
59 of the best songs that brought in the new millennium: Accidentally in Love • Beautiful • Don't Know Why • Get the Party Started • Hey Ya! • I Hope You Dance • 1985 • This Love • A Thousand Miles • Wherever You Will Go • Who Let the Dogs Out • You Raise Me Up • and more.
00311186 .... $24.95

ACOUSTIC ROCK
Over 70 songs, including: About a Girl • Barely Breathing • Blowin' in the Wind • Fast Car • Landslide • Turn! Turn! Turn! (To Everything There Is a Season) • Walk on the Wild Side • and more.
00311747 .... $24.95

THE BEATLES
Over 90 of the finest from this extraordinary band: All My Loving • Back in the U.S.S.R. • Blackbird • Come Together • Get Back • Help! • Hey Jude • If I Fell • Let It Be • Michelle • Penny Lane • Something • Twist and Shout • Yesterday • more!
00311389 .... $24.95

BROADWAY
Over 90 songs of the stage: Any Dream Will Do • Blue Skies • Cabaret • Don't Cry for Me, Argentina • Edelweiss • Hello, Dolly! • I'll Be Seeing You • Memory • The Music of the Night • Oklahoma • Summer Nights • There's No Business Like Show Business • Tomorrow • more.
00311222 .... $24.95

CHILDREN'S SONGS
Over 110 songs, including: Bob the Builder "Intro Theme Song" • "C" Is for Cookie • Eensy Weensy Spider • I'm Popeye the Sailor Man • The Muppet Show Theme • Old MacDonald • Sesame Street Theme • and more.
00311823 .... $24.99

CHRISTMAS
Over 100 essential holiday favorites: Blue Christmas • The Christmas Song • Deck the Hall • Frosty the Snow Man • Joy to the World • Merry Christmas, Darling • Rudolph the Red-Nosed Reindeer • Silver Bells • and more!
00311241 .... $24.95

COUNTRY
96 essential country standards, including: Achy Breaky Heart • Crazy • The Devil Went down to Georgia • Elvira • Friends in Low Places • God Bless the U.S.A. • Here You Come Again • Lucille • Redneck Woman • Tennessee Waltz • and more.
00311296 .... $24.95

JAZZ STANDARDS
99 jazz classics no music library should be without: Autumn in New York • Body and Soul • Don't Get Around Much Anymore • Easy to Love (You'd Be So Easy to Love) • I've Got You Under My Skin • The Lady Is a Tramp • Mona Lisa • Satin Doll • Stardust • Witchcraft • and more.
00311226 .... $24.95

LOVE SONGS
Over 80 romantic hits: Can You Feel the Love Tonight • Endless Love • From This Moment On • Have I Told You Lately • I Just Called to Say I Love You • Love Will Keep Us Together • My Heart Will Go On • Wonderful Tonight • You Are So Beautiful • more.
00311235 .... $24.95

LOVE STANDARDS
100 romantic standards: Dream a Little Dream of Me • The Glory of Love • I Left My Heart in San Francisco • I've Got My Love to Keep Me Warm • The Look of Love • A Time for Us • You Are the Sunshine of My Life • and more.
00311256 .... $24.95

MOVIE SONGS
94 of the most popular silver screen songs: Alfie • Beauty and the Beast • Chariots of Fire • Footloose • I Will Remember You • Jailhouse Rock • Moon River • People • Somewhere Out There • Summer Nights • Unchained Melody • and more.
00311236 .... $24.95

ROCK
Over 80 essential rock classics: Black Magic Woman • Day Tripper • Free Bird • A Groovy Kind of Love • I Shot the Sheriff • The Joker • My Sharona • Oh, Pretty Woman • Proud Mary • Rocket Man • Roxanne • Takin' Care of Business • A Whiter Shade of Pale • Wild Thing • more!
00311390 .... $24.95

TV SONGS
Over 100 terrific tube tunes, including: The Addams Family Theme • Bonanza • The Brady Bunch • Desperate Housewives Main Title • I Love Lucy • Law and Order • Linus and Lucy • Sesame Street Theme • Theme from the Simpsons • Theme from the X-Files • and more!
00311223 .... $24.95

WEDDING
83 songs of love and devotion: All I Ask of You • Canon in D • Don't Know Much • Here, There and Everywhere • Love Me Tender • My Heart Will Go On • Somewhere Out There • Wedding March • You Raise Me Up • and more.
00311309 .... $24.95

FOR MORE INFORMATION, SEE YOUR LOCAL MUSIC DEALER, OR WRITE TO:

HAL•LEONARD CORPORATION
7777 W. BLUEMOUND RD. P.O. BOX 13819 MILWAUKEE, WI 53213

THE BEST OF CONTEMPORARY CHRISTIAN MUSIC

The ancient Greek "sign of the fish" (Ichthys) is an instantly recognizable Christian symbol in pop culture. It is used on car bumpers, clothing, jewelry, business logos, and more. Hal Leonard is proud to offer The Fish Series, showcasing the wide variety of music styles that comprise the Contemporary Christian genre. From the early pioneers of CCM to today's biggest hits, there's something for everyone!

CHRISTMAS (Green Book)
40 Contemporary Christian holiday favorites, including: Christmas Angels • Christmas Is All in the Heart • He Made a Way in a Manger • Joseph's Lullaby • Manger Throne • Not That Far from Bethlehem • 2000 Decembers Ago • While You Were Sleeping • and more.
00311755 P/V/G.................................$19.95

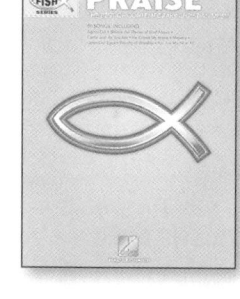

PRAISE (Yellow Book)
50 songs of praise and worship, including: Agnus Dei • Before the Throne of God Above • Come Just As You Are • He Knows My Name • Majesty • Open Our Eyes • Worthy of Worship • You Are My All in All • and many more.
00311759 P/V/G.................................$19.99

EARLY YEARS (Orange Book)
41 songs, including: The Day He Wore My Crown • Father's Eyes • I Wish We'd All Been Ready • Love Crucified Arose • Rise Again • Sing Your Praise to the Lord • Who Will Save the Children • Your Love Broke Through • and more.
00311756 P/V/G.................................$19.99

ROCK (Black Book)
41 rock hits from some of the biggest names in Contemporary Christian music, including: All Around Me • Count Me In • Everlasting God • I'm Not Alright • Meant to Live • No Matter What It Takes • Tunnel • Undo • and more.
00311760 P/V/G.................................$19.95

INSPIRATIONAL (Blue Book)
42 songs of encouragement and exaltation, including: Call on Jesus • Find Your Wings • God Will Make a Way • Healing Rain • Jesus Will Still Be There • On My Knees • Say the Name • Your Grace Still Amazes Me • and many more.
00311757 P/V/G.................................$19.95

WEDDING (White Book)
40 songs from Contemporary Christian artists for the bride and groom's big day, including: Cinderella • God Knew That I Needed You • Household of Faith • I Will Be Here • Look What Love Has Done • A Page Is Turned • This Day • Without Love • and more.
00311761 P/V/G.................................$19.99

POP (Red Book)
44 top pop hits from favorite Contemporary Christian artists, including: Always Have, Always Will • Brave • Circle of Friends • For Future Generations • If We Are the Body • Simple Things • To Ever Live Without Me • What It Means • and more.
00311758 P/V/G.................................$21.95

WORSHIP (Purple Book)
50 songs perfect for a worship band or solo praise, including: Amazing Grace (My Chains Are Gone) • Beautiful One • Days of Elijah • Forever • In Christ Alone • Mighty to Save • Revelation Song • Sing to the King • and many more.
00311762 P/V/G.................................$21.95

HAL • LEONARD® CORPORATION
7777 W. BLUEMOUND RD. P.O. BOX 13819 MILWAUKEE, WI 53213
Visit Hal Leonard Online at
www.halleonard.com

Prices, contents and availability subject to change without notice. Prices listed in U.S. funds.